ISONOMIA *and the* ORIGINS OF PHILOSOPHY

ISONOMIA

and the

ORIGINS OF PHILOSOPHY

....

KŌJIN KARATANI

Translated by Joseph A. Murphy

DUKE UNIVERSITY PRESS · *Durham and London* · 2017

TETSUGAKU NO KIGEN

BY KŌJIN KARATANI

© 2012 by Kōjin Karatani

Originally published 2012 by Iwanami Shoten,
Publishers, Tokyo

This English edition published 2017 by Duke
University Press, Durham, NC, by arrangement
with the proprietor c/o Iwanami Shoten,
Publishers, Tokyo.

© 2017 Duke University Press

All rights reserved

Printed in the United States of America on
acid-free paper ∞

Designed by Matthew Tauch

Typeset in Scala by Graphic Composition, Inc.,
Bogart, Georgia

Library of Congress Cataloging-in-Publication Data

Names: Karatani, Kōjin, 1941– author.

Title: Isonomia and the origins of philosophy / Kōjin
Karatani ; translated by Joseph A. Murphy.

Other titles: Tetsugaku no kigen.

English Description: Durham : Duke University Press, 2017.
| Includes bibliographical references and index.

Identifiers: LCCN 2017004990 (print) | LCCN 2017011334 (ebook)
ISBN 9780822368854 (hardcover : alk. paper)
ISBN 9780822369134 (pbk. : alk. paper)
ISBN 9780822372714 (e-book)

Subjects: LCSH: Philosophy, Ancient.

Classification: LCC B115. J3 K3713 2017 (print) |
LCC B115. J3 (ebook) | DDC 180—dc23

LC record available at https://lccn.loc.gov/2017004990

Contents

Chapter 4

POST-IONIAN THOUGHT

Chapter 5

SOCRATES AND EMPIRE

APPENDIX

Translator's Note

···············

This translation is based on the fourth edition of *Tetsugaku no kigen* (Iwanami Shoten, 2012). The text incorporates extensive quotation from Greek, German, Japanese, French, and Chinese sources. Where available, accepted English-language translations have been used. Where not available, translations have been adapted from web-based sources, or translated from the original, as indicated in the citations. I would like to acknowledge the advice and assistance I received from the author's wife, Lynne Karatani, which has been instrumental to the project's readability.

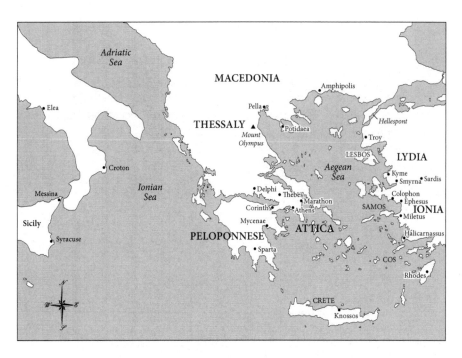

MAP 1 — Map of the Ionian and Aegean Sea Region

Author's Preface to the Japanese Edition

....

In the process of writing my last work, *Sekaishi no kôzô* (Iwanami Shoten, 2010; translated as *The Structure of World History*, Duke University Press, 2014), it occurred to me that I should give more detailed consideration to ancient Greece. However, considering the overall balance of the work, it seemed better advised to place these thoughts in a new volume. This book is the result. Consequently, it takes the theoretical framework presented in *The Structure of World History* as a premise. Still, even without that knowledge, this book should be easy enough to follow. To be on the safe side, though, I have included a summary of the argument of *The Structure of World History* and notes on how that corresponds to this book, as an appendix called "From *The Structure of World History* to *Isonomia and the Origins of Philosophy*." In points where the argument of this book is unclear, please refer to this text.

The first version of this book was serialized in the monthly journal *Shinchô*, to whose chief editor, Yutaka Yano, I owe a great debt. Without his support, this work would never have come to fruition. I am similarly indebted to the editor of this book, Kiyoshi Kojima, from Iwanami Shoten.

KŌJIN KARATANI · SEPTEMBER 15, 2012 · BEIJING

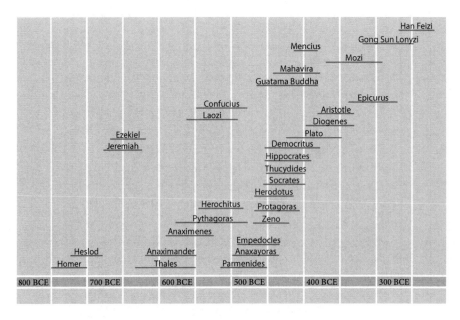

FIGURE INTRO.1 — Chronology of Ancient Greek and Asian Thinkers

Introduction

....

UNIVERSAL RELIGION

Around the sixth century BCE, Ezekiel and the biblical prophets emerged from among exiles in Babylon; Thales emerged in Ionia on the coast of Asia Minor; Gautama Buddha and the Jain founder Mahavira appeared in India; and Laozi and Confucius emerged in China.[1] This simultaneity and parallelism are striking and cannot be explained straightforwardly based on socioeconomic history. As an example, Marxists typically see philosophy and religion as parts of an ideological superstructure, itself determined by the economic base, by which is meant the modes of production. However, attention to transformations of the economic base has not proven sufficient to explain the overall dramatic transformations of this period.

Consequently, a perspective that would explain the transformations of this period as a revolution or evolution of spirit taking place at the level of the ideological superstructure became dominant. This view is best represented by Henri Bergson's *The Two Sources of Morality and Religion* (1932). According to Bergson, human society started as a small closed society, and morality developed out of it for its benefit. If so, what might have transpired for it to become open? It is clear that in the time leading up to the sixth century BCE, human society was evolving at multiple locations from clan society to world empire, where diverse peoples interact on the basis of trade. But this by itself is not sufficient to bring about an open society. For Bergson, "Never shall we pass from the closed society to the open society, from state to humanity, by any mere broadening out. The two things are not of the same essence."[2] Bergson tried to understand these transformations at the level of religion. According to him, religion in a closed society is static, while religion in an open society is dynamic. The leap from static religion to dynamic religion is brought about by the "individual of privilege." Bergson argues that *elan d'amour*, or an "impetus of love," is at the basis of the evolutionary transformations, and manifests itself through the actions of these individuals of privilege.

However, we need not, and should not, appeal to this kind of theoretical leap. I acknowledge that the leap from a closed society to an open society occurred on the level of religion. Having said that, this fact itself can be traced to the economic base, in my opinion, on the condition that we understand the economic base in terms of modes of exchange, instead of the Marxist's usual modes of production. For example, the development of religion—from animism, to magic, to world religion, finally to universal religion—falls out neatly when understood in terms of transformation in the modes of exchange.

Normally, the term *exchange* implies commodity exchange. I refer to this as mode of exchange C. This arises when exchange occurs between one community and another, not in exchange internal to a community or family. What occurs in the latter is reciprocity in the form of the gift and repayment, which is mode of exchange A. There is a further type of exchange, different from both, called mode of exchange B. This is an exchange between the ruler and the ruled, which at first glance does not appear to be a kind of exchange. However, if the ruled, in offering obedience to the ruler, receives protection and security in return, this too is an exchange. The state has its roots in this mode of exchange B.

The historical transformations of religion can be tracked in terms of these changes in the mode of exchange. For example, in animism, all things in the world are each thought to possess an *anima* (or spirit). Because of this, a person cannot associate with an object without first putting its anima under control. For example, a person cannot take an animal in hunting without this accommodation to the anima. In this case, the person despiritualizes and objectifies the anima, first by means of making an offering to it and imposing debt on it. This is what is called sacrifice. Burial and funeral rites, as well, accommodate the anima of the dead person through an offering. Magic, too, is a mechanism of this kind of exchange, based on gift giving. It is about putting nature under the magician's control by making it into an inanimate object by means of a gift to its anima. If understood in this way, magicians, who see nature as an object, can be regarded as the first scientific thinkers.

An important point here is that, in the society of nomadic hunter-gatherer bands, we find the pure gift but not the reciprocal exchange. There is animism but not magic. Because both reciprocity and magic are attributes of closed societies, it follows that the closed society and corresponding static religion took shape only after fixed settlements arose. The earliest nomadic societies were not in fact closed societies. These were not something that naturally existed from the outset. Closed society emerged in a leap when faced with the crisis brought about by fixed settlements. Fixed settlements brought about accumulations of wealth and power that had not hitherto been possible, and with this the emergence of class divisions and the state. We may be able to say that clan societies imposed reciprocity as a duty on their members in order to avoid these divisions.

To repeat, magic was developed in the tribal societies that emerged after fixed settlements. The fixing of settlements resulted in the need for people to coexist with a myriad of others, both living and dead. As a result, magical arts developed, alongside obligations of reciprocal exchange, and the status of the chief priest ascended. But this ascent happened in a decisive way in state societies. Whenever a centralized state emerges from conflict among city-states, the power of the king-priest is solidified, along with which gods become transcendent.

If we consider this development in terms of modes of exchange, a despotic state is a situation where mode of exchange B is dominant. However, even in this case, both king and subject regard this as a reciprocal relation (mode of exchange A), rather than a relation of the ruler and the ruled, where active submission and rendering of tribute on the part of the subject makes the security and redistributive action of the state appear a gift. The same can be said about the relation between gods and humans.

In a despotic state, gods are rendered transcendent, in domination over humans, while at the same time the reciprocal relationship between gods and humans from the preceding magical stage lingers. The logic there goes something like this. The gods are transcendent and beyond the grasp of the human mind. However, if people offer gifts and prayers, the gods will be obliged to respond to their requests. In this type of relation, the transcendent character of the gods is not yet fully established. For example, if the state were to be defeated, the gods would be discarded.

After this stage, conflicts among various states produce over time a state that rules over a vast territory, or world empire. World empire requires not just military dominance, but the establishment of a trading bloc over a vast area (mode of exchange C). The god in this case becomes a world god that transcends the old tribal gods and tutelary deities. Still, at this stage, universal religion is yet to appear. Because, here again, the god would be abandoned if the empire were to be defeated. A world empire, then, is a necessary but not sufficient condition for the emergence of universal religion.

Universal religion too could be understood based on the mode of exchange. To put it simply, universal religion is an attempt to recuperate mode of exchange A at a higher level, after it has been dissolved by modes B and C. To put it in other terms, when a society based on the principle of reciprocity is dismantled by the permeation of state rule and a money economy, universal religion seeks to reinstate those relations of reciprocity and mutual support on a higher level. I call this mode of exchange D.

Mode D seeks to reconstitute A on a higher level. However, D cannot be realized without the prior negation of A. From a different perspective, this means the negation of the magical phase in religion. In this sense, Max Weber is right in locating the defining characteristic of universal religions in "disenchantment." Disenchantment is generally understood to happen in relation to the rise of the natural sciences; however, for Weber disenchantment lies in the negation of the idea that the gods can be bent to human will by rituals and prayers: "Religious behavior is not worship of the god, but rather coercion of the god, and invocation [of the god] is not prayer, but rather the exercise of magical formulae."[3] It is in the loosening of the hold of the idea of coercion of the gods that a scientific attitude toward nature becomes possible.

In terms of modes of exchange, Weber's disenchantment implies that reciprocity in the relations between humans and gods is renounced. In fact, to carry this out is not as easy as it seems; even in today's world religions, coercion of the god continues to be practiced in the form of prayer. If this coercion was really to be renounced, it would be nothing less than a world historical event. However, it is not sufficient to attribute such an event to the appearance of a particular individual of privilege, who opens the closed society.

So, how did coercion of the gods come to be set aside? We can discover an example in the establishment of Judaism. The Old Testament narrates the history of the Israeli people, from the covenant "between God and the people," to the exodus led by Moses from Egypt, to the development of the state by David and Solomon after settling in Canaan. However, the codification of the Old Testament was initiated in the Babylonian exile, and the history written there is largely a restructuring, or creation from whole cloth, of events from the perspective of that time. That is to say, Judaism as a universal religion was established among the exiles in Babylon, themselves taken from the fallen kingdom of Judah, and projected backward to its origins.

The Jewish people started as a nomadic tribal confederacy. They gathered under the single god Yahweh, and made covenant with this god. However, this is no anomaly. We see the same process among the cities of Mesopotamia and the Greek poleis. When a number of villages or tribes join to form a single city-state, this takes the expression of conjointly following a new deity. This is a type of social contract. We have, then, no reason to regard the covenant of the Jewish people as exceptional.

The Jewish tribal confederacy formed in response to the presence of powerful nations (Egypt and Assyria) all around them. In other words, the confederacy was formed as a means of resisting external polities. However, once the Jewish people settled in the land of Canaan and started to engage in agriculture, they experienced a fundamental change in lifestyle from their nomadic origins. What was heretofore a tribal federation was eventually transformed under the reign of David and Solomon into an "oriental despotism" similar to the order of Egypt. That the people would switch their allegiance from the Yahweh of the nomadic peoples to the agricultural god Ba'al could be said to be the natural course of events.

In the age of Solomon, God was rendered transcendental, reflecting the expansion of the royal authority. However, this was still little more than an extension of the tribal deity. Transcendental though this God may be, were the people to be vanquished in battle, he would be discarded. This signifies a relation where the people, while placing themselves in a position of obedience, still feel entitled to coerce reciprocity from God through offering gifts. In other words, this religion remained essentially magical.

Abandoning of God actually happened, upon the fall of the northern kingdom of Israel, which was established as the result of the split of the kingdom of Solomon after his death. God was abandoned yet again upon the consequent fall of the second kingdom, the southern kingdom of Judah. However, something unprecedented occurred among the people taken into captivity in Babylon from Judah. Though vanquished in battle and their nation lost, rather than repudiate their god, an inversion occurred whereby responsibility for events was sought on the human side. This is a decisive break with coercion of the gods and signals the disenchantment of religion. Here the rejection of reciprocity between God and humans brought about a fundamental shift in their relationship. But in another sense, the relation of human to human was also fundamentally changed.

The people taken to captivity in Babylon were largely members of the elite and literate classes, and generally engaged in commerce. Away from home in Babylon, separated from the older administrative structures including religion, and separated from their agricultural communities, they lived as individuals. It was just such individuals who came to form a new covenant community under God. This took expression as a covenant between God and the people. This resembles the process of formation of a nomadic tribal confederacy but is different. And it is also different from the thought of the biblical prophets active in the dynastic age.

These prophets criticized oppression by the bureaucracy and priesthood, the degenerate character of the people, and disparities in wealth, warning that the nation would perish if such things persisted. However, their message aimed at restoration of the old nomadic tribal order, a return to the desert—that is, a restoration of mode of exchange A, or a reciprocal community. This kind of prophet is not particular to the Jewish religion. Any place where a nomadic people were turned to agriculture under a despotic rule, and faced with the crisis of communities and nation, this kind of prophet calling for a return must have appeared. However, the call for a return to mode A by itself does not immediately lead to universal religion.

The arrangement that emerged in Babylon was a covenant community of free and equal individuals, released from tribal constraints. We can understand this as the recuperation of mode of exchange A on a higher dimension, that is to say, mode of exchange D. The recuperation at a higher dimension requires not only the negation of modes B and C, but the negation of mode A itself. That is to say, what is required first is for people to be released from tribal society and the state. These conditions were granted by the captivity.

The Jewish exiles in Babylon were released about forty years later by the Persian Empire, after its defeat of Babylonia, and returned stateless to Jerusalem. From that point forward, the Jewish sect was transformed into a mechanism for governing the stateless people. In other words, the covenant community in Babylon was transmuted into a collective regulated by priests and scribes. The compilation of the Old Testament was further advanced at this time. Through this process, the words of the prophets, the legend of Moses, and so forth were given new meaning.

The compilation of an authorized scripture was carried out by the Jewish sect from the perspective of theocracy and was rearranged so that all laws would appear as if based in the word of God handed down to Moses. Through this process, the captivity in Babylon was cast as little more than an episode in the long history of the Jewish religion or the Jewish peoples. In this way, Babylon, the true origin of Judaism, was erased. Along with this, the fact that Judaism, once a universal religion, had fallen back to a conventional religion ruled by a priestly authority was also forgotten. As a result, Judaism came to be identified with the religion of the Jewish people.

In truth, Judaism continued to spread up to the time of Roman rule. This was not really a matter of population growth among the Jews. Rather, Judaism as a universal religion attracted many converts. For example, the sect that sprang up around Jesus grew as one faction in Judaism. They formed a collective, which was itinerant and communistic. We see a similar development in other sects that emerged at the time, such as, for example, the Essenes. These nomadic religious movements of Judaism sought to recover the covenant community of the age of Babylon.

EXEMPLARY PROPHETS

It might appear from the discussion to this point that universal religion was disclosed solely by the Jewish prophets or those in that lineage. That is not the case. In relation to this, a distinction drawn by Weber is suggestive. Weber divides prophets into two types: ethical and exemplary. In the former, as with the Old Testament prophets, the prophet is inspired by God and becomes a medium to proclaim God's will, demanding that people obey God, as part of the ethical obligations entailed in that trust. In the latter type, as with Buddha, Laozi, or Confucius, the prophet is a standard to which other people aspire, who points out to people the path to religious salvation through his own example. In this way, contrary to common understanding, Weber is able to subsume some thinkers not normally thought of as religious into the category of prophets, and by doing so put the usual definition of world religion in brackets.

This leads to a further bracketing of the standard classifications of religion and philosophy. The usual distinction is that philosophy is rational, while religion is nonrational or beyond reason. Further, philosophy is Greek in origin and religion Hebraic. However, such divisions thwart our understanding not just of philosophy but of religion.

For example, the prophets of Israel spoke the word of God. However, these in fact were the words of humans. That is to say, these were not mystical communications from a sacred realm, but intellectuals reporting as the word of God realizations they had reached after passing through certain trials of understanding.[4] Meanwhile, as to the origins of Greek philosophy, they are usually located in the natural philosophy of Ionia. This was a critique of the gods of Olympus by means of reason. Hence, it is generally understood that philosophy began as the antithesis of religion. However, Ionian natural philosophy was not atheism. It is true that these philosophers criticized the anthropomorphic gods, but such a critique was possible precisely through the acquisition of the concept of a nonanthropomorphic "one God." As with universal religion, natural philosophy came into being through a process of disenchantment. Hence, it is not plausible that those philosophers limited their inquiries into nature in a narrow sense. In this sense, Ionian natural philosophers could even be regarded as exemplary prophets.

The concept of the exemplary prophet is necessary to look at the world-historical leap that occurred simultaneously around the sixth century BCE. Philosophy appeared in Ionia at virtually the same time as universal religion appeared in Israel. In order to examine the universal significance of this simultaneity, we need to look at yet another unprecedented intellectual phenomenon arising around the same time in East Asia.

In China, the Hundred Schools of Thought became active in the Spring and Autumn period, or Warring States period. Thinkers of the Hundred Schools would travel from city to city expounding their thoughts. The condition for the receptivity of these thinkers was that it had become untenable for city-states to rely solely on the conventional wisdom of clan societies. The Hundred Schools included figures such as Laozi, Confucius, and Mozi, Legalists represented by Han Feizi, the Logicians (alternately School of Names) represented by Gong Sun Longzi, and others. In terms of contemporary disciplines, the Legalists would fall under political philosophy, and the Logicians linguistic philosophy. However, this kind of classification is meaningless. The leap that occurred in this period cannot derive exclusively from any of these categories. What is important is rather the simultaneous and competitive emergence of diverse ways of thinking.

Laozi and Confucius, though they would enter history as founders of Daoism and Confucianism, were not particularly religious themselves. It is clear that Laozi's idea of *wu wei ziran* (nonaction/naturalness) bears no relation to Daoism's later inclination toward magic, because wu wei or nonaction is nothing other than a negation of the coercive and magical relation to the gods.[5] Similarly in the *Analects* we find, "Of portents, wonders, and heavenly beings, the Master passes over in silence," and "not yet even knowing life, how can one seek to know death?" Confucius, however, was neither an atheist nor a skeptic. It was simply a renunciation of the magical posture of coercion of the gods. Confucius believed in a transcendent heaven. However, this belief had prompted him rather to transfer the focus of his philosophy to the relation of person to person in this world.

Meanwhile, Laozi developed the concept of *dao*, or the Way. Dao, in its literal sense a material object, signifies the infinite here. What Laozi effected was a form of natural philosophy. This was also a political philosophy. Just as those who inherited the legacy of Ionian natural philosophy advocated doubting *nomos* (man-made order) and following *physis* (nature), Laozi's natural philosophy had direct political implications.

If we consider this from the perspective of modes of exchange, Laozi's thought is first a rejection of mode A, or restrictive communities. It is, second, a rejection of mode B, or rule by force. In the midst of the Spring and Autumn period, when states and communities were collapsing around him, Confucius sought to rebuild them through "benevolence," which means a return of mode A. Laozi rejected even benevolence; "When the Great Way falls into disuse, benevolence becomes the fashion." "The Great Way" implies what is akin to the way of the world of nomadic peoples prior even to mode A. Then, the idea of wu wei ziran, nonaction and naturalness, can be said to point to mode of exchange D.[6]

The teachings of Laozi and Confucius were taken in later years to have opened the way for new religions. However, in both cases they were free thinkers who refused the course of religions up to that point. In this sense, there is no difference between them and the prophets of Israel or the natural philosophers of Ionia. As long as we follow the contemporary classifications that separate religion, philosophy, and science, we will never be able to recognize the world-historical leap in the sixth and fifth centuries BCE. What they mark, in each case, is the emergence of mode of exchange D into human history. My effort to rethink the birth of "philosophy" in Ionia is for these reasons.

Chapter 1

Ionian Society and Thought

ATHENS AND IONIA

Buddha and Laozi were free thinkers, who appeared at a time when ancient societies were at a turning point. They later came to be regarded as religious founders, but we would do better, rather, to reexamine them as free thinkers. On the other hand, what I would like to attempt here is to take a group of free thinkers roughly contemporary to them in the Ionian city-states, and the set of thinkers who inherited their legacy, and reexamine them as exemplary prophets.

It is common practice today to locate in Ionian natural philosophy forms of thought that anticipate modern science, while disregarding other aspects. It is as if Ionian thinkers dealt exclusively with the physical world and were indifferent to things outside that domain, as are most scientists today. This picture, however, is a prejudice put in place by Athenian philosophers who came later such as Plato and Aristotle. For example, in *Phaedo*, Plato gives credit to Socrates for shifting the focus of philosophy from inquiry into the external world to the aims of human behavior in society. Aristotle as well characterized philosophers before Socrates as natural philosophers, and claimed that with the appearance of Socrates, philosophy first turned its attention to inquiry into ethics. This is to imply that philosophy in a true sense began in Athens, and whatever existed in Ionia only played the role of foreshadowing.

Their perspective remains with us today and is not easy to overturn, because we have very few surviving documents of the Ionian thinkers other than the accounts given by Plato and Aristotle. As long as we rely on these accounts, we will only be able to see what is selected out through their conception of philosophy. In order to free ourselves of this prejudice, it is first necessary to place this Athenocentric perspective in doubt.

In fact, nearly all of what is believed to be distinctive about Greece began in Ionia. For example, the revision of Phoenician glyphs to produce an accessible alphabet is often posited as a contributing factor in Greek democracy. This process began in Ionia. The works of Homer too, a fount of Greek culture, are written in Ionian dialect. The use of the market, rather than bureaucratic fiat, to regulate prices is also regarded as a contributing factor in bringing about Greek democracy. This too is an Ionian development. It was the Ionians who adopted the technology of coining money from neighboring Lydia and, as a result, Ionia became one of the very first to develop foreign trade and a money economy.

The technology, religion, and thought of Egypt, Mesopotamia, and the ancient Near East intersected in Ionian cities. The people of Ionia actively integrated these new ideas and developments, but at the same time never integrated certain systems developed in the Asiatic despotic states, such as, for example, bureaucracy and standing or mercenary armies. Unlike these despotic Asian states, the Ionians did not fix commodity prices according to state bureaucracy, but rather left it to the market. After being developed in Ionia, this system spread to other regions.

The same applies to the principles of the polis. It is typically claimed that, in contrast to older clan societies defined by kinship, the Greek polis was constituted by autonomous individual choice. However, this type of principle did not apply uniformly throughout the Greek poleis. The principle first appeared in the early colonial cities in Ionia, and expanded from there through further colonization from those cities. It was only later that the principle spread to the Greek mainland.

The poleis on the Greek mainland began as tribal confederations. For example, Athens was based on social strata that went from household (*oikos*) to clan (*genos*) to brotherhood or kinship (*phratry*) to the tribe (*phylai*), of which there were originally four. Athens was no longer a clan society as such; however, its tribal traditions were still alive and well. What dissolved these traditions and made the people into a *demos* were the reforms of Cleisthenes in 508 BCE. However, that did not prompt the formation of the kind of polis, based on an autonomous social contract by individuals, that would transcend claims of kinship. For example, in the age of Pericles, often regarded as the zenith of Athens, citizenship was determined by kinship, and foreigners (people from other poleis) were excluded.

The Athenian polis in this sense was not fundamentally different from city-states outside the Greek territories, which were in their nature tribal confederacies. The process by which ceaseless conflict among city-states, themselves constituted as tribal confederations, ends up in the establishment of a despotic state is visible throughout Mesopotamia, Egypt, and ancient China. The same process is evident in the tribal confederacy of Israel, which, as I previously outlined, resulted in forming an Asiatic despotic state in the reigns of David and Solomon. It was only after the kingdom's destruction at the hands of Babylonia, and during the captivity in Babylon, that Judaism acquired the principles to reject this path.

The Greeks, by contrast, did not follow this course. It is not enough to point to the semiperipheral position of Greece, or its persistent attachment to tribal customs. The Mycenaeans and the Cretans who preceded the Greeks in populating the region did follow this course, passing through a stage of conflict among many small city-states (small kingdoms) to the formation of an Asiatic despotic state. That is in fact the usual course of affairs. It was certainly possible that the Greek people moving southward into the peninsula after the Mycenaean collapse would follow the same path. However, what happened instead was that a number of autonomous poleis were formed.

Why would that be? It must be because they were possessed of a principle that disallowed the formation of the state. This is a different matter from saying they retained the principles of a tribal society. Certainly, tribal society resists formation of a state. However, once they accept civilization, there is an inevitable turn toward an Asiatic despotic state. At this point, instead of working against the process, tribal principles work to reinforce it. Nevertheless, the Greek peoples' migration anew into the Attic peninsula did not turn in this direction. Rather, while severing the hold of tribal principles, they recovered on a higher level antistatist tendencies inherent in the tribal society.

This phenomenon arose in Ionia, among the large numbers of immigrants from Athens and the Greek mainland. And what happened in this land stands with what happened in Babylon as an experience unparalleled in world history. Neither Ionia nor Babylon is neglected in historical accounts. However, their epoch-making significance has been buried. Without Ionia, the culture and politics of Athens likely never would have been. We would have to say, rather, the Athenians, while undergoing the continuous influence of the politics and thought of Ionia, tried strenuously to repress them. Athenian philosophy, in a word, was an attempt to overcome ideas of Ionian origin while incorporating them. And this attempt was not merely a philosophical problem, but political as well.

<hr/>

ISONOMIA AND DEMOCRACY

The development of democracy in Greece is usually recounted with Athens as its center. This, however, is a mistake. It needs rather to be seen from Ionia. However, in another sense, such a view is right. That is to say, what we call democracy did not exist in Ionia. What existed in Ionia was not democracy but *isonomia*. Democracy and isonomia are two different things, but typically seen as synonymous. Herodotus's use of isonomia in *The Histories* is no exception. In my experience, the only person to distinguish the two, and assign this difference its proper importance, is Hannah Arendt:

> Freedom as a political phenomenon was coeval with the rise of the Greek city-states. Since Herodotus, it was understood as a form of political organization in which the citizens lived together under conditions of no-rule, without a division between rulers and ruled. This notion of no-rule was expressed by the word *isonomy*, whose outstanding characteristic among the forms of government, as the ancients had enumerated them, was that the notion of rule (the "archy" from αρχειν in monarchy and oligarchy, or the "cracy" from κρατειν in democracy) was entirely absent from it. The *polis* was supposed to be an isonomy, not a democracy. The word *democracy*, expressing even then majority rule, the rule of the many, was originally coined by those who were opposed to isonomy and who meant to say: What you say is "no-rule" is in fact only another kind of rulership; it is the worst form of government, rule by the demos.
>
> Hence, equality, which we, following Tocqueville's insights, frequently see as a danger to freedom, was originally almost identical with it.[1]

Arendt seems to understand this principle of isonomia to be present throughout Greece. However, if we accept her position, many contradictions arise. As I discuss later, even according to her own logic, the origins of isonomia have to be assigned to Ionia. Isonomia (no-rule) was not simply an idea but a living reality in the city-states of Ionia. It was only after the fall of the Ionian states to the Lydian empire in the sixth century that it spread to other regions as an idea.

Why did isonomia, or no-rule, arise in Ionia? This is because among the migrants of Ionia, existing clan and tribal traditions were severed, constraints and privileges set aside, and a new type of covenant community (*schwurgemeinschaft*) launched. The Spartan or Athenian poleis, by contrast, were formed as tribal confederations, and older tribal traditions were still deeply entrenched. These resurfaced as inequality or class antagonisms within the polis. If one were to seek to implement isonomia in such a situation, it could only be through rule by democracy, or the principle of majority rule.

In Ionia, people were free from traditional ruling relations. There, isonomia was not just an abstract idea of equality. People were in fact economically equal in their lives. Although a monetary economy was developed there, this did not lead to disparities in wealth. I will explain its reasons later, but, to put it simply, in Ionia a landless person could simply migrate to a new city, instead of working on someone else's land. Naturally, this left no room for great landowners to emerge. In that sense, we could say freedom gave rise to equality.

By contrast, the advance of a monetary economy brought about serious class disparity in the poleis of the Greek mainland, with a great number of citizens falling into indentured servitude. In Sparta, in order to keep this adverse development in check, trade and the money economy were abolished and economic equality strictly enforced. This equality came at the expense of freedom. In Athens, on the other hand, while preserving their freedom and the market economy, a system was developed whereby the impoverished majority used the power of the state to force a redistribution of the wealth of the minority. This is Athenian democracy.

Aristotle writes, "The basis of a democratic state is liberty . . . and one principle of liberty is for all to rule and be ruled in turn."[2] In this sense democracy might appear to be no-rule. However, people are not equal in wealth. Hence Aristotle continues, "Every citizen, it is said, must have equality, and therefore in a democracy the poor have more power than the rich, because there are more of them, and [what the majority decides] is supreme."[3] In other words, democracy is majority rule. Equality, in this case, is brought about by constraints on the liberty of the aristocratic minority. Then the argument cannot be made that Athenian direct democracy, unlike modern representative democracy, escapes the conflict between freedom and equality. Rather, all the problems inherent in the modern democracy are exposed here.

Modern democracy is a composite of liberalism plus democracy, that is to say liberal democracy. It attempts to combine, therefore, two conflicting things, freedom and equality. If one aims for freedom, inequalities arise. If one aims for equality, freedom is compromised. Liberal democracy cannot transcend this dilemma. It can only swing back and forth like a pendulum between the poles of libertarianism (neoliberalism) and social democracy (the welfare state).

It is widely thought that in liberal democracy humankind has arrived at its ultimate form, and there is nothing left for us but trying to make moderate progress within its limitations. Needless to say, however, liberal democracy is nothing of the sort. There remain ways to transcend it. Further, it is possible to discover a key to this in ancient Greece, but by no means are we talking about Athens. Taking Athenian democracy as a model will never allow us to solve the problems of modern democracy. It is more important rather to recognize in Athens the prototype of these problems.

It was Carl Schmitt who observed that modern democracy was composed of a liberalism and democracy that were themselves contradictory. Nowadays democracy is understood to be synonymous with parliamentary democracy; however, democracy is possible without the parliamentary system. According to Schmitt, the parliamentary system is not intrinsic to democracy, but rather to liberalism. "Democracy requires, [rather], first homogeneity and second—if the need arises—elimination or eradication of heterogeneity."[4] Consequently, "Bolshevism and Fascism, as with all totalitarian forms, are anti-liberal, however it does not necessarily follow that they are anti-democratic."

In terms of ancient Greece, Sparta was a kind of state socialism, while Athens was a kind of liberal democracy. In contrast to Sparta, where individuality was sacrificed for the sake of economic equality, Athens recognized a market economy and freedom of speech, but to that degree had to face inequality and class division. Athenian democracy was a system that sought to equalize the people by redistribution of wealth. On the other hand, this democracy was rooted in the homogeneity of its members. It excluded heterogeneity. These are the aspects reinforced in the age of Pericles, taken to be the golden age of the Athenian system.

Athenian democracy was realized not only by relying on the exploitation of slaves and resident foreigners, but on the subjugation of other poleis as well. For example, Pericles used the Delian League to divert monies confiscated from other poleis in order to alleviate economic disparities among Athenian citizens, distributed as a per diem when they attended the assembly. That is to say, Athenian direct democracy was enabled by imperialist expansion. Direct democracy gave rise to demagogues, who inflamed the people. Looked at in this way, while one can discern in Athens the contradictions that vex contemporary democracy today, to seek the key to their solution there would be clearly off the mark.

ATHENIAN DEMOCRACY

The cities of Ionia were successively subjugated beginning in the midsixth century BCE, first by Lydia (under Croesus) and then Persia (under Cyrus). By the end of the sixth century, most cities were ruled by tyrants appointed by the Persian Empire. Athens, on the other hand, had brought down its own tyranny and, with the reforms of Cleisthenes in 508, was moving toward a democracy. The Ionians were emancipated by Athens through their participation in the Greek victory over Persia. As a result, even in Ionia, Athens had come to be regarded as the shining pioneer of the democratic system. *Isonomia* remained as a word, but it had lost the sense it once had in Ionia.

As an example, Herodotus in *The Histories* uses the term *isonomia* several times, but regards it as synonymous with Athenian democracy. Though Herodotus was himself from Ionia, he was raised at a time when the Ionian city-states had long been under the rule of Persia, and isonomia had become an abstraction indistinguishable from the democracy he encountered in Athens.

By the time of the Athenian Thucydides, almost no interest in Ionia is shown. For example, in the *History of the Peloponnesian War*, he refers to the Ionian cities as having been formed by migrants from Athens. However, this was a view that arose only after the Persian War, when the Athenian empire had brought the Ionian territories under its rule.[5]

In fact, the people that established the colonies in Ionia came not just from Athens but from all over the region. Moreover, the Ionians did not place great importance on ties with their place of origin. This has led to the establishment of a unique culture, free from deep attachment to the traditions of the tribal society that characterized the mainland. By the seventh century BCE, it was widely known even in the mainland that Ionia had developed trade and manufacturing to a high degree, and that something called isonomia existed there.

Athenian democracy is understood to have begun with the reforms of Solon, who designated himself *archon* in 594 BCE. In order to help the commoners who had fallen into indentured servitude, Solon forgave all extant debts, freed indentured servants, and forbade the use of a person as collateral for debt. He further created an assembly in which all citizens were expected to participate and granted citizenship to resident foreigners. However, it is not plausible that Solon thought these measures up by himself. He rather learned them from Ionia. Hence, Solon was the first Athenian who attempted to implement isonomia. However, he was to be frustrated in this attempt.

Solon was soon supplanted by the tyrant Peisistratus. He had warned the citizens of Peisistratus's designs, but in vain, and ended up in exile. However, the fact that isonomia was not realized in Athens was because the kind of social conditions present in Ionia were lacking. In Athens, there was a stark gap between the landholding nobility and the common citizen. Without economic equality, the political equality of isonomia remains a lifeless idea. And this equality can only be realized by the confiscation and redistribution of land. In fact, this is what the masses demanded, and it was the tyrant Peisistratus (ruling 560–27 BCE) who fulfilled their demands.

After this, the tyranny in Athens continued until 510 BCE, after which democracy is generally regarded to have begun in earnest. This is not exactly wrong. However, tyranny and democracy do not differ as starkly as it might appear. Solon criticized the tyrant Peisistratus as being against isonomia. However, Peisistratus's position was that the measures taken by Solon were insufficient to realize isonomia, and securing it would require passing through a dictatorial power to effect the redistribution of land through it. Hegel observed that Solon lacked insight as a politician, and that we need to look at Solon and Peisistratus as a pair who collaborated by taking up two different tasks:

Communal law, insofar as the individual does not discern or comprehend its meaning, is bound to appear to the individual as violence. . . . It is required at first to exercise force, then as a result of this force, insight is born in the people, and the law appears, not as something imposed from the outside, but as arising from themselves. The majority of lawgivers and administrators of state accepted the need to exercise force on the people and to become tyrants. For the reason that, if they did not accept this charge, another individual would appear to undertake it, it was an unavoidable state of affairs. . . . The tyranny of Peisistratus accustomed the Athenians to the laws of Solon, and brought them into usage, so that after this usage came to be general, tyranny was superfluous; his sons were hence driven out of Athens, and for the first time the constitution of Solon upheld itself. Solon undoubtedly gave the laws, but it is another thing to make such regulations effectual in the manners, habits, and life of a people. These two tasks divided among Solon and Peisistratus were united in Periander in Corinth, and Pittacus in Mitilene.[6]

According to Hegel, this was the understanding that Solon lacked: to wit, that his aims could only be realized by passing through the dictatorship of Peisistratus, not by his own measures. However, Hegel himself overlooks the following point. If we grant that what Solon aimed for was isonomia, in Athens this ultimately remained unrealized. It is true that after Peisistratus's death, the tyranny was abolished and democracy set in motion. However, this democracy was a form of rule different in kind from the no-rule of isonomia.

What Hegel discerned in Athens was rather the political process of modernity. Modern democracy has been realized by a twofold process. First, an absolute monarchy or developmental dictatorship appears and brings under control the various forms of feudal power, and then these themselves come to be toppled by bourgeois revolution. The fact that realization of democracy requires a concentration of power as its prerequisite reveals that democracy essentially takes the form of a -cracy or rule. In modern democratic revolution, the old sovereign (the king) is either killed or banished, and the heretofore subjugated peoples become sovereign. But in fact, in this people-as-sovereign, absolute monarchy is concealed. In other words, democracy is a form of rule realized by passing through the concentration of power.

The Ionian city-states fell because they did not have sufficient military power for their own defense. They stressed trade and manufacture, and did not place great store in military matters. The Athenians, on the other hand, like the Spartans, were fundamentally warrior-farmer communities, who prioritized military matters. As a money economy developed in Ionia, it also penetrated to the city-states of the Greek mainland, where, however, the citizenry did not engage in commerce and manufacture. The penetration of the money economy devastated these warrior-farmer communities, as more and more citizens fell into indentured servitude. This very quickly led to a military crisis for the city-states whose defense hinged on self-armed hoplite citizens. Consequently, social reform came to be considered indispensable for the continued existence of the polis. The nobility had no choice but to assent.

The motive for the promotion of democracy in Athens lay in this military exigency. This was completely different from the process by which isonomia was established in Ionia. On the other hand, democratization also took place in Sparta. Here it took the form of a flat abolition of trade and the money economy, and the equalization of land ownership. In a sense, this is the most thoroughgoing of the democracies. However, the Spartan state was premised on the subjugation of the neighboring Messenians and their reduction to *helots*, or state-owned slaves, whose labor and the fertility of their territories rendered external trade unnecessary. In exchange for this, the Spartans had to be constantly prepared to face helot rebellion, and thereby arose the need to solidify themselves as a community of warriors. From there was born Spartan militarism.

In Athens, by contrast, abolishing trade and the money economy was unfeasible. The only open path was to incorporate these while trying to solve the resulting class problems. This is what democracy is. Athenian democracy, in this sense, was first and foremost required for the survival of the state. That is to say, military matters demanded democracy. The phalanx tactics employing heavily armed infantry adopted from the mid-seventh century BCE were completely different from the older cavalry tactics of the mounted nobility, whereby they rode horses and commoners were foot soldiers. The nobility were rendered marginal as a result. The phalanx tactic hastened the formation of democracy not just in Sparta but in Athens as well. Further, while warships on the Persian side in the Persian War were rowed by galley slaves, on the Greek side, by contrast, they were rowed by commoners too poor to arm themselves properly. Further, with victory in the war, the political status of these poor commoners was further strengthened.

In other words, while Ionian isonomia took shape as part of the development of independent farming, trade, and manufacture, Athenian democracy took shape solely for military reasons, or in response to the demands from a warrior-farmer class. In Athens, democracy in the strict sense of the term was brought about through the reforms of Cleisthenes in 508 BCE after the death of Peisistratus and the lapsing of the tyrants that succeeded him. It was through these reforms that something called the demos (as in democracy) first appeared. Concretely speaking, Cleisthenes reorganized the old tribal system that was the basis of the power of the nobility and established new tribal affiliations based on region. With this, a demos with a territorial character is produced. This implied on the one hand the rejection of kinship-based clan society, while seeking a return to the tribal principle of reciprocity. In this sense, one might say the demos of ancient Greece resembled Benedict Anderson's idea of the modern nation as imagined community.

Athenian democracy is inseparable from this kind of nationalism. In Athens, no matter how wealthy a foreigner might be, he could neither own land nor become a citizen. Further, despite not being protected under the law, he was still subject to heavy taxation. Further, the Athenian citizens were by formal status farmers, but few were engaged in the actual labor of agriculture. In order to prosecute wars, and participate in political affairs, they had to rely on slaves for labor. A landowner with no slaves would be unable to carry out the obligations of a citizen. Slaves were, in this sense, a condition for citizenship. Hence, the development of democracy necessitated even more slaves. Unlike the citizens of Ionia, the citizens of Athens scorned manual labor as the work of slaves. The difference between the thinkers of Ionia and the thinkers of Athens is nowhere more stark than in this fact.

In ancient Greece, hundreds of poleis were jumbled together, forming and reforming leagues while engaged in ceaseless conflict. This was an unparalleled state of affairs. Marx sought the cause of this in the fact that Greece attained a high level of civilization while keeping in place tribal social systems. "That they were able to preserve the old clan (*genos*) organization for such a long time, from the settlement in Attica to the time of Solon, is due chiefly to the unsettled conditions and incessant warfare of the tribes (Attic)."[7]

It is true that the social systems of clan society were deeply entrenched in the poleis on the Greek mainland, exemplified by Athens and Sparta. For example, rule by noble lineage rooted in the old tribal groups remained. However, the principles that gave Greek poleis their distinctive character did not originate here. As outlined before, the city-states that sprang up at multiple points in the ancient world, after passing through an extended period of rivalry and conflict, typically resulted in the formation of an Asiatic despotic state. The reason the Greek states did not follow this path did not lie in the persistence of the principles of clan society. Quite the contrary, it was because there was a principle capable of negating this. This was the idea of isonomia that came from Ionia.

Why Ionia? In a word, because the cities of Ionia were formed by colonists, who did not bring with them the tradition of the clans. The settlers there were freed from the bonds and restraints of kinship. This meant that they were severed from the kind of reciprocal principle that demanded, simply by the fact of being born in a place, that in the face of a gift an individual was obligated to offer repayment. There is no contradiction here with their fidelity to the polis. Rather, these settlers voluntarily chose to become members of the new polis. The Ionian polis came into being with a covenant (social contract) among these people. Their fidelity was directed not to kinship but to the covenant.

Their covenant was made under oath to Apollo or the other gods of Olympus. Consequently, fidelity to the polis took the form of a fidelity to the gods. It is important to note here that the gods of the Ionian polis were not the tutelary gods of the old tribal groups but the foreign gods of Olympus. The place in Greece where the principles of the polis were first secured was not the mainland, where the old clan social organization persisted, but rather the colonial cities, where they were absent. It was only later that these principles were transmitted to Athens and other poleis.

What is clear from the foregoing is that the originality of the Greek polis was created through the active colonizing activity from roughly 1000–800 BCE. The crucial point here is the manner of colonization. The new communities formed by the settlers in Ionia were independent from the city-states or tribal groups of their origin. From Miletus and other poleis, then, further migration occurred. This serial colonization then ended up rendering null the ties to the old tribal traditions.

As a rule, migrants retain ties to the mother country or city-state. Relying on these ties, the state sends out colonists to expand its territory. This was the case with the Roman Empire. However, when colonial cities are closely tied and subordinated to the originating city, colonial activity becomes a measure for territorial competition among the cities of origin and, ultimately, under the pressure of such competition the conditions for the contending poleis to coexist are lost. As we know, a single city emerged victorious in Italy and built the Roman Empire. Hence, for the colonial cities to lose their ties to the mother city and tribal tradition, as we see in Greece, is not the general case.

Why did such a state of affairs emerge in Greece? It was not because Greece had an advanced civilization. Quite the opposite; social customs of the old tribal groups were very much alive in the Athenian mainland. And in fact, the process of colonization among the Greek city-states was similar to that in other tribal societies. For example, Morgan identifies a general mechanism in discussing the North American tribal societies. "When a village became overcrowded with numbers, a colony went up or down on the same stream and commenced a new village. Repeated at intervals of time several such villages would appear, each independent of the other and a self-governing body; but united in a league or confederacy for mutual protection."[8]

In the clan societies that develop along with fixed dwellings, deep inequalities and internal antagonisms arise as a result of growth and expansion. Colonization was a mechanism for relieving this pressure. The anthropologist Alain Testart framed the problem this way: "In nomadic hunter-gatherers, the flexibility, divisibility and fluidity of the social structure did not permit exploitation beyond certain permissible limits. If such did arise, the exploited parties would simply move on to another place, and the band would split. Consequently, collective decisions had to be reached through unanimous agreement. Under conditions of fixed settlement, the structure of fixed dwellings and storage became factors inhibiting the free movement of people. Dissatisfied people could no longer simply leave, opening the way for more serious exploitation."[9]

Clan society, which if left to itself becomes a sedentary society with deep class divisions, maintained equality by a strict system of reciprocity. However, there are limits to this as well, so occasionally some members migrate to other places. One could well say that the nomadic principle is recovered for clan society through colonization. Further, new clans are typically formed through migrant settlers, enabling their association. These associations further associate and form tribal federations.

This was the nature of colonial activity in Greece as well. The multiple poleis born from this process, while they did engage in mutual warfare, were forming loose confederations as exemplified in the Olympic games. The impetus for this lay in migration to Ionia. These gave birth to a new principle. In a sense, the colonies of Ionia from the Greek mainland based themselves in the principles of clan society. Consequently, in Ionia, no control was exercised from the mainland. However, exactly for that reason, in Ionia, the old tribal social principles that bound the individual were negated.

As a result, what was restored in the cities of Ionia was the nomadic existence that preceded tribal society. Obviously, this is not to say the Ionians became hunter-gatherers or nomadic herdsmen. They recuperated nomadism by the practice of foreign trade and manufacturing. This was to discard the warrior-farmer tradition prevalent in Greece. Herodotus writes of the customary scorn of the Greeks for the "skilled trades" and "handicrafts" as follows:

> Whether the Greeks borrowed from the Egyptians their notions about trade, like so many others, I cannot say for certain. I have remarked that the Thracians, the Scyths, the Persians, the Lydians, and almost all other barbarians, hold the citizens who practice trades, and their children, in less repute than the rest, while they esteem as noble those who keep aloof from handicrafts, and especially honor such as are given wholly to war. These ideas prevail throughout the whole of Greece, particularly among the Lacedæmonians. Corinth is the place where mechanics are least despised.[10]

In fact it would be better to say that the skilled trades or handicrafts were least despised in Ionia. However, by the time of Herodotus this character had lapsed. What I would like to emphasize here, though, as Herodotus points out, is that the scorning of the skilled trades and handicrafts is characteristic of a culture that values the plundering and coercion of others into labor. What is set in motion in Ionia, by contrast, is a culture that values life based on labor and exchange. But why did this not give rise to class divisions? Put differently, why was it there that the principle of isonomia, where equality is realized through freedom, could be established?

It is usually believed that the incursion of a money economy gives rise to class divisions. And in reality, as the market economy developed in Athens, a great number of citizens fell into debt servitude. The democratization of Athens, beginning with the reforms of Solon, was meant to deal with this situation. The same holds true for the abolition of the money economy under the communism of Sparta. However, a money economy does not immediately lead to large landholdings or class division. It is not the mere fact of trade that brings this about; it is the system that forces others into labor. Without the labor power of slaves, or debt servitude, the concentration of wealth and large landholdings cannot become established.

In Ionia, on the other hand, a farmer who cultivated his own land was the norm, and there were no large landholders. The reason is that in Ionia, others available for employment did not exist. Persons without land simply left for a new place, instead of remaining in place to work another's land. In addition, by contrast with Athens and Sparta, Ionia did not rely on slave labor. The large-scale acquisition of slaves, and consequent need to prevent rebellions and escapes, required a militarist state. However, Ionia did not take that path. They actively pursued a life of commerce, trade, and manufacture.

In Ionia, the progress of commerce, manufacturing, and trade did not bring about serious class disparities. A money economy gives rise to disparities in wealth only where there are disparities in political power. For example, huge profits can be obtained from overseas trade when this is monopolized by the state. In general, trade with distant lands is carried out by the state. This may be conducted by bureaucrats or left to merchants and managed through taxation. Athens was no exception. Trade was left to resident foreigners, from whom taxes were collected. Although

Athens flourished as the center of trade, the citizens themselves did not engage in commerce. Their accumulation of wealth was based on the slave labor of the mines and the farmers' fields.

Ionian trade, on the other hand, which extended throughout the Asian region, was not national but private, carried out through networks of merchants and manufacturers. The Ionian polis, in a sense, was essentially a council for these merchants and manufacturers. When a state monopoly is absent, there is a leveling of the profits from trade. Accordingly, trade and the market economy do not immediately give rise to disparities in wealth. The reason class divisions multiplied under the money economy in Athens was that from the outset political power was held by a landowning nobility.

That kind of inequality, and ruler-ruled relation, did not arise in Ionia. That is to say, isonomia obtained. If in a given polis such inequality and the ruler-ruled relation did arise, people could simply move to another place. In this sense, the ability to move is a fundamental precondition of isonomia. In addition to this, yet another kind of mobility was brought to Ionia by the growth of commerce and manufacture.

To put it in terms of modes of exchange, in Ionia modes A and B were transcended by mode C, and with this as a premise, the nomadic mobility at the basis of mode A was recuperated in a higher dimension. This is mode D, that is to say isonomia, where equality is realized through freedom. If we take Athenian democracy to prefigure contemporary liberal democracy (parliamentary democracy), Ionian isonomia provides the key to a system that would transcend it.

ICELAND AND NORTH AMERICA

There are almost no historical or archaeological materials to give us an idea what Ionian cities were really like. There are two possible approaches to make inferences. First, we can read the work of the Ionian thinkers. Even if the fragments are not explicitly political, if we can discern in this work something that would have been impossible without the social system particular to Ionian cities, it becomes indirect evidence. The second method is to draw inferences in world history from cases that resemble Ionia. In this section, we begin by pursuing the latter.

For example, the independent city-states of the European Middle Ages or Renaissance would appear to resemble the Greek polis. And in fact, the renaissance of ancient Greece arose there. However, there is a significant difference between the two. The independent city-states of Europe were established with the sanction of the Church and the feudal lords, and in these cities, democratization advanced through struggles against the church and the nobility. The subjects of this movement were the guilds, such as the *Zunft* in German cities, and the *popolo* in Italy. One could say this resembles the process of democratization in Athens. However, the Ionian poleis were nothing like either of these. There the rule of priests and tribal nobility was absent from the start. The principle of isonomia in Ionia arose first and foremost as a natural result of colonization and immigration, which happened without ever going through the process of democratization or class struggle.

From this perspective, two points of reference may be useful in thinking about the Ionian polis. One is the Icelandic Commonwealth from the tenth to the thirteenth century CE. Settlers there established an autonomous society of farmers, who cultivated their own lands. There was neither sovereign, nor central government, nor military, and all matters were decided by the Althing, an assembly of farmers. Catholicism was adopted in the tenth century; however, unlike the practice in other regions, the priests did not act as authorities and were in most cases married. Class inequalities and the setting of person over person did not exist in any sense. All these allow us to say that there existed isonomia.

We find nothing comparable to this type of society in all the cities of Europe, much less their contemporary Scandinavian countries. And it was not material conditions that led to this formation. Iceland had no industries beyond livestock and no external trade. One might think the society established in Iceland could be explained in terms of being underdeveloped, but this was not the case either. Europe in this period was still governed by a strong tribal consciousness, which underlaid the feudal system, but we find not a trace of this in Iceland. One point of evidence is that, despite themselves being from northern Europe, the people of Iceland produced a literature different in kind from the northern European tradition of mythology and epics of heroic deeds, the arguably modern Icelandic sagas. These were less oral tradition than creative literature, and while they detail the conflict among chiefs, are nothing like the epic tales of valor and bravery. They employ a thoroughly realistic depiction and further depict men and women on an equal footing.

The Icelandic sagas bear absolutely no resemblance to the European heroic epics but in some ways resemble the poetry of Homer, born in Ionia. The Homeric epics sing the praises of the valor and martial exploits of great heroes, but at the same time are filled with cries of lamentation and resentment against them. As with Homer's poetry, born of Ionian society, Icelandic sagas too arose from an isonomic society. Moreover, it is conjectured that the Norse legends derived from the spread of Greek legends to northern Europe. In Iceland, however, the northern European gods are withdrawn from the scene. In this sense, the Icelandic sagas bear a curious connection to Ionian natural philosophy, in its rejection of the Greek gods, and to the Ionian society that allowed such thoughts.

How did such a society come about? The only possible explanation is that it was formed by migrant settlers. The Icelandic Commonwealth was built between 870 and 930 CE by immigrants from Norway, who eventually numbered on the order of ten to twenty thousand. Further, this was not a systematic colonization from a central state; rather, individual settlers came haphazardly, one after another. Naturally, no bond was carried over from the Norwegian state or tribal communities. More accurately, they emigrated out of distaste for them. Their place of origin in Norway was the quintessential aggressive state built by the Vikings. Iceland, by contrast, was formed through a social contract among individuals who rejected this state. Because of this, though lacking in terms of productive power, Iceland stood out as singularly isonomic in contemporary European society.

We can find the second example of an isonomia that resembles that of Ionia in the American townships of the eighteenth century. Here again we have a society formed by the unsystematic arrival of settlers from older, class-based societies. Of course, the process of immigration and city formation were not uniform throughout North America. These were divided according to whether migrants retained deep ties to their country of origin or not. For example, Spanish and French colonies were extensions of the mother country. Here plantations were the main form of settlement, and when labor did not suffice, slaves would be purchased from Africa. No such situation arises, on the other hand, among the English colonies. This was because England had already gone through their civil war and bourgeois revolution (1647–49). With the exception of levying taxes, England showed little inclination to interfere with the American colonies and also allowed settlers from outside England.

America's particular system of civil society was developed in the British colonies on the Eastern Seaboard. This was called the township. Here, when settlers joined the town, they would be given a fixed amount of land. A citizen could in theory own more land than this, but in practice this was virtually impossible, because even if one did lay hold of a large tract of land, no excess labor could be obtained to work it outside of the family. If a person didn't own land, he did not need to work someone else's; he simply set out for the frontier. Again, if one was dissatisfied with the politics of the town, one could simply leave. In short, the mobility (freedom) of its members brought about equality. All these allow us to say that the township was a kind of isonomia.

Towns were governed by a council (town meeting) and had a self-administered judicial system. The town itself did not expand. Rather, while maintaining autonomy, towns federated in a bottom-up process with other towns and formed counties. Counties then federated with other counties to form states. This kind of federated system is often said to show the influence of Montesquieu. However, as I will outline, this system was in place well before the revolution that produced the United States.

The experience of Iceland and the American townships gives us clues to discern the conditions that allowed the Ionian polis to come into being. First, and most important, there had to be enough frontier land available to enable free movement. This results in a state of affairs where it is freedom itself that maintains equality. Moreover, trade and manufacture were developed based on the ethos of the independent farmer, who values labor. Another condition is that Ionian cities experienced no threat of aggression from neighboring nations. Of course Lydia existed nearby; however, until the time of Croesus it was not an aggressive state, and the Ionian cities were able to secure peace and independence merely by paying tribute. It was just so with the American states, securing their autonomy from the English simply by paying taxes.

As we have seen, isonomia as township requires both internal and external conditions for being. Should these conditions cease, the polity will either cease to be or transmute to another form. For example, in 1262 Iceland was subjugated by Denmark and disappeared as an autonomous society. However, as was the case with the fall of the Ionian poleis, its collapse was not solely due to external invasion. The gradual incursion of class partition was the root factor.

In the case of preindependence America, open space for new arrivals was the indispensable precondition for the maintenance of the townships. When this space ran out, colonies resorted to the occupation of Native American lands. However, this measure was put to a halt by England. In 1763 a ruinous rebellion was led by the Native American chief Pontiac, and England concluded a treaty with the native tribes that halted expansion westward beyond the Appalachian range. Those who were planning on westward expansion were indignant at the suppression of their expansion, and from this point calls for political independence heightened. In order to maintain the autonomous development of the townships, independence from England became essential. This required the formerly federated state organizations to solidify. As a result, through the American Revolution, what had until then been a federation of towns was transformed into a centralized state, leaving the townships or federalism in name only.

Mobility (freedom to move) brings about equality. However, in order to maintain this equality, there must be an expansion of space that guarantees mobility. Here is the contradiction inherent in the isonomia or township of a federated system. The American Revolution was carried out in order to preserve the federated townships, but at the same time deprived them of their essence. The city-states of Ionia, on the other hand, were never federated. Hence, they were unable to resist the incursions of the neighboring states of Lydia or Persia. Herodotus describes the situation as follows:

> It was while the Ionians were still in distress, but still, amid it all, held their meetings, as of old, at the Panionium, that Bias of Priêné, who was present at the festival, recommended (as I am informed) a project of the very highest wisdom, which would, had it been embraced, have enabled the Ionians to become the happiest and most flourishing of the Greeks. He exhorted them "to join in one body, set sail for Sardinia, and there found a single Pan-Ionic city." . . . Before their misfortunes began, Thales, a man of Miletus, of Phœnecian descent, had recommended a different plan. He counseled them to establish a single seat of government, and pointed out Teos as the fittest place for it; "for that," he said, "was the center of Ionia. Their other cities might

still continue to enjoy their own laws, just as if they were independent states." This also was good advice.[11]

In short, according to Herodotus, Thales counseled formation of federation of the poleis in order to escape subjugation by the Persians, but was unable to gain consensus. As a result Ionia fell. Incidentally, this example hints at how inadequate it is to reduce Thales's production to statements such as, "the origin of all things is water," as well as how intimately Ionian natural philosophy was tied to political matters.

<hr/>

ISONOMIA AND COUNCIL

Thales emerged as a natural philosopher in his later years, just when Miletus was coming under the sway of Lydia. In regard to this Hegel says, "As regards the external and historical condition of Greece at this time, Greek philosophy commences in the sixth century [BCE] in the time of Cyrus, and in the period of decline in the Ionic republics in Asia Minor. Just because this world of beauty which raised itself into a higher kind of culture went to pieces, Philosophy arose. . . . At the time of the decline in Ionic towns, the other Greek states ceased to be under its ancient line of kings."[12]

As to what this "world of beauty" of the Ionic republics, "which raised itself into a higher kind of culture," might actually have been, Hegel is silent. Still, his argument that Ionian philosophy emerged exactly as the republics were collapsing is suggestive. This means, in our context, that philosophy arose in the crisis of isonomia. This crisis did not come solely from the exterior. There must have been internal factors too. That is to say, that Thales's idea to form a federation was frustrated indicates that in most of the poleis in the region, isonomia had already collapsed.

When isonomia was a living reality, the Ionians took it for granted, and did not try to rationalize or theorize it. That we have so few documents attempting to explain isonomia should be sought in this fact. We find a similar instance in the absence of a great deal of rationalization and theorization of the townships among the colonists of the Eastern Seaboard in North. The idea of the townships became an important political idea only after its spirit had been lost with the War of Independence.

The direct democracy of the township, which did not recognize majority rule, collapsed after the Revolution and transmuted into the representative democracy of the centralized state. It was Jefferson in particular who acutely felt this as a threat to republicanism. Hannah Arendt calls attention to Jefferson's call to "partition counties" into wards:

So the republic, according to Jefferson, would not be secure in its very foundations without the ward system. Had Jefferson's plan of "elementary republics" been carried out, it would have exceeded by far the feeble germs of a new form of government which we are able to detect in the sections of the Parisian Commune and the popular societies during the French Revolution. However, if Jefferson's political imagination surpassed them in insight and in scope, his thoughts were still travelling in the same direction. Both Jefferson's plan and the French *sociétés révolutionaires* anticipated with an utmost weird precision those councils, *soviets* and *Räte*, which were to make their appearance in every genuine revolution throughout the nineteenth and twentieth centuries. Each time they appeared, they sprang up as the spontaneous organs of the people, not only outside of all revolutionary parties but entirely unexpected by them and their leaders. Like Jefferson's proposals, they were utterly neglected by statesmen, historians, political theorists, and, most importantly, by the revolutionary tradition itself. Even those historians whose sympathies were clearly on the side of revolution and who could not help writing the emergence of popular councils into the record of their story regarded them as nothing more than essentially temporary organs in the revolutionary struggle for liberation; that is to say, confronted them with an entirely new form of government, with a new public space for freedom which was constituted and organized during the course of revolution itself.[13]

Why Arendt did not connect this council to isonomia does not make sense to me, despite her having already delineated the concept of isonomia in this same book. Perhaps she regarded isonomia as characteristic not of Ionia, but of Athens, or Greece generally, as has become standard since Athens became the center of Greece. By that time Ionia had already been forgotten. Hence even Herodotus, raised in Ionia and deeply influenced by Ionian thought, equates isonomia with the democracy current in Athens. It seemed never to have occurred to him that isonomia was not just another means of ruling, but "a new space of public freedom, forged and organized through the process of revolution itself."

Just as Ionia fell into oblivion with the rise of Athens as the center of Greece, the significance of the American Revolution, itself a product of the township, was pushed into disregard, not just by the outside world, but among the Americans themselves. "Less spectacular perhaps, but certainly no less real, are the consequences of the American counterpart to the world's ignorance, her own failure to remember that a revolution gave birth to the United States."[14]

Of the two revolutions that occurred at roughly the same time in the late eighteenth century, it is almost exclusively the French Revolution that has exerted influence worldwide. Arendt locates the reason in the "poverty" emphasized as a motive in the French Revolution, a motive absent in the American Revolution. The American Revolution, which occurred in a "povertyless society," did not exert the same subsequent influence as the French. In fact, as serious class divisions developed in the United States from the nineteenth century on, it was revolutionary thought arising from the French Revolution that gained influence.

Incidentally, Arendt's povertyless society is not the same as a wealthy society. It means a society with little disparity in wealth. As delineated before, in the American townships, because a person with no land could simply move to another space, it was nearly impossible to support large landholdings. In other words, this system lacked the conditions for the accumulation of wealth made possible by employing other people. Naturally, class division did not emerge there. The same applies to Iceland and to Ionia as well.

In Athens, by contrast, the gap between rich and poor widened under the rule of the old noble houses. It was in this circumstance that the revolution of the tyrant Peisistratus occurred. It is typically thought that democracy is established through the rejection of tyranny. However, a tyrant is required to put in place the plan for the equitable distribution of land. And even in a post-tyrannical democracy, other tyrants and demagogues often arise. The force that drove Athenian democracy was essentially the problem of poverty. This was the kind of democracy that the French Revolution recapitulated. The American Revolution, on the other hand, is rooted in an isonomia of the farmers, who cultivated their own land. Such roots, though, were ignored and buried in oblivion by the Americans themselves. This is because there too, democracy quickly gained the upper hand.

Incidentally, Arendt is perceptive of this amnesia with regard to American townships; however, she is unaware of the same amnesia in regard to Ionian isonomia. The same can be said of the understanding of the Greeks in Heidegger, who was her teacher. According to Heidegger, the being of an entity was repressed in philosophy after Socrates. However, this perspective does not go beyond the romantic notion that in a modern society, people have forgotten the communal mode of existence. If we would still talk about a forgetting of being, we should rather locate it in the Athenians' complete erasure of the primordial isonomia that existed in Ionia.

Heidegger's position lies basically in the inheritance of the Nietzschean critique of the loss of direct intuition and the tragic sensibility in post-Socratic philosophy. Nietzsche made reference to the pre-Socratic philosophers; however, he did not pursue the question of how profoundly they were tied to Ionia and its spirit. What Nietzsche felt was lost in post-Socratic Athens was not the legacy of Ionia, but the Athenian tradition of the warrior-farmer communities. This position is a mere projection of his contemporary Romantic view of history onto Greece.

Chapter 2

The Background of Ionian Natural Philosophy

NATURAL PHILOSOPHY AND ETHICS

What we know about the philosophers of Ionia is largely passed down through Plato and Aristotle. As a result, it is shaped by the philosophical perspective created by them. According to this account, whereas the Ionian philosophers directed their inquiry to the nature of the natural world, Socrates turned his inquiry toward the aims of human behavior in society. That is to say, Ionian thinkers thought about nature, but not about problems of ethics or the self. That view, however, is simply a misconception.

Ethics is concerned with the question of how the individual is to live. However, when fixed in relation to the community, the individual does not exist in a real sense. It is by severance from the community that one first becomes an individual. Then, for the first time, the self is discovered and the question of ethics arises. In this sense, Ionia was the first in the Greek region to raise the question of the self and ethics. In Athens at the time, no such questions presented themselves. This is because the Athenian people were not yet individuals, independent from community affiliations present since the stage of clan society.

Ionia, on the other hand, was composed of colonists from various communities; hence the individual existed from the start. The Ionian polis was established through the social contract among such individuals. Here, at the same time one was free from traditional community bonds, one was loyal to a polis one had chosen. This fidelity was based purely on individual will, not on the accident of birth. This is why, should inequality arise within the polis, one could simply leave. Isonomia as a principle can only be realized under these conditions.

In Athens, the conditions were different. The Athenian polis was also formed through a kind of contract among its members. However, this was an agreement among tribes, and not a social contract among individuals. People were derivative of their clans. Naturally, with the penetration of a money economy, individuals or individualism arose in Athens too. And at this point finally they began engaging isonomia and the natural philosophy of Ionian origin. However, in Athens these were considered a threat to traditional communities and were the target of ceaseless attack. Natural philosophy, with its rejection of the gods of the polis, was viewed as a denial of the polis (community) itself. And so, for Anaxagoras, a close friend of Pericles for many years, the charge that earned him banishment from Athens was sacrilege against the gods. Sometime later, Socrates would be executed for the same reason.

Plato and Aristotle place great emphasis on the epoch-making novelty of Socrates. However, this is not because Socrates discovered something different from Ionian thought. Rather, he was the first to catch hold of its significance and put it into practice. That is to say, Socrates was the first person in Athens to attempt to lead his life as an individual. In that sense he was *cosmopolitan*, independent from the polis and the community of Athens. But at the same time, he was the first person whose membership in Athens as a polis was based, not on the accident of birth, but on a voluntary decision. This could be why, though he could have escaped his punishment, Socrates chose to remain in Athens and accept death.

Plato and Aristotle saw Socrates as a martyr for the sake of his native community, and sought to vindicate Socrates by differentiating him from the Sophists, who were mostly nonnative Athenians with whom he had been identified. However, Socrates is better understood as a Sophist from Athenian soil, fundamentally within the lineage of the Ionian thinkers. Nonetheless, Plato ascribes his own theory of ideas to Socrates, and in *Sophists* mounts his own attacks on the Ionian materialists under Socrates's name, likening it to the legendary battle of the gods against the titans. One could say that Plato's battle against Ionian natural philosophy was his lifelong mission.

Socrates, however, differed from Plato. The real lineage of Socrates's thought should be traced less through Plato than through such individualist and cosmopolitan thinkers as Socrates's direct disciple Antisthenes, founder of the Cynics, and Antisthenes's disciple Diogenes. According to Diogenes Laërtius's *Lives of the Philosophers*, Antisthenes rejected the theory of ideas, remarking once at a parade, "Plato, I see a horse, but I do not see horseness." Diogenes, when asked what country he hailed from, replied, "I am a citizen of the world [cosmopolite]." These remarks allow us to infer that Socrates should be seen as a cosmopolitan, who rejected the theory of ideas. This means that far from standing in opposition to the Ionian school, as Plato pictured it, Socrates should rather be placed in its lineage.

The Ionian thinkers were of the polis. As much as they were advocates of a cosmopolitan and universal ethics, they sought to realize these in their chosen polis. In this sense they were political, that is to say, literally of the polis. Hence it misses the mark to categorize the Ionian natural philosophers as limiting their thinking to the natural world, as when Aristotle refers to Thales as a physician (phusiologoi). Prior to that, Thales had been widely known rather as a sage (sophoi), who was active as a technologist, mathematician, and politician. Considering this, it does not seem right to limit his Sophia, or wisdom, to a physics.

The same can be said of Thales's young friend Anaximander. Versus Thales's location of the element from which all things derive (the arche) in water, Anaximander is known for finding the arche in the indefinite or boundless (apeiron). But Anaximander's interests were also not limited to physics, and he engaged at the same time in inquiries into history and comparative civilizations. For example, in his surviving fragments we find studies of the orthography of the Greek alphabet, observations on geography, and so forth.[1] In the same period, Hecataeus, a historian and geographer of Miletus, is known to have carried out a critique of the mythological nature of the account of history in the Homeric narratives. However, in this case too, history and geography should be regarded as part of natural philosophy in a broad sense.

One can locate the same points in Democritus, regarded as a terminus of Ionian natural philosophy—though I would personally locate this in Epicurus. Democritus was a prolific writer, but little remains to us but fragments. Among those fragments, few touch on matters explicitly outside the scope of natural philosophy, but the following are representative:

Man as a microcosm . . . [1]

Avoid wrongdoing not for fear, but out of duty. [2]

Many, who have learned little of reason, still live according to reason. [3]

He would rather discover one causal explanation than obtain the whole Persian Empire. [4]

The whole earth is open to the wise man. For a noble soul has the whole world as its native country. [5]

Poverty in a democracy is clearly preferable to so-called prosperity under tyranny. Just so is freedom preferable to slavery. [6][2]

It is not difficult to discern here an ethicality that we do not find in Athenian philosophers. In Athens, people are subordinate to the polis, and all ethics flows from that point. However, for Democritus, a human being is in essence independent of the polis, and each person is "a world unto themselves" (*microcosmos*). Hence for Democritus, true ethics cannot come from within the polis but rather only from the *cosmopolis*. However, this is not an ethics worthy of the name for Athenian philosophers. From their perspective, ethics is lacking not just in Democritus but in Ionian thinkers in general. This is why their thought is considered a physics, prior to Athenian philosophy.

It does indeed seem that Ionian philosophers wrote very little beyond their meditations on external nature. However, this does not indicate a lack of interest in ethics and politics. They rather expressed their understanding of ethics and human existence from the standpoint of physis. In their eyes, the world and human beings were themselves equally physis or nature. They were among the first to propose this universal perspective. It is precisely this approach I would like to call natural philosophy. In my understanding, this is inextricable from Ionian politics (i.e., isonomia).

Before turning to Thales, Anaximander, and other so-called natural philosophers, I would like to take up two later figures, the physician Hippocrates and the historian Herodotus, who embody the Ionian tradition of ethical and political thought, and who appear unlikely in the context of Athens. They clearly illustrate that a new kind of ethics, different from the rules of the poleis, was present in Ionian natural philosophy. Both these figures were raised in cities to the south of Ionia. These were places where Ionian intellectual traditions remained active even after Ionia had been brought under Persian rule.

In *Herodotus in Context*, Rosalind Thomas makes the case that Herodotus (484–425 BCE) was keenly interested in the particulars of medicine, health, and clinical practice, and was acquainted with parts of Hippocratic medicine, and seeks to read from this fact the intellectual climate of "East Greece" (i.e., Ionia and its regions to the south) that nurtured those figures:

> But as I hope we have seen, Ionian and East Greek tradition (if we can include those who wrote in Ionic as in the same intellectual tradition) were thriving in the latter part of the fifth century. It was moving into new subject areas, above all, medicine, and spreading beyond Ionia and the East Aegean coast. The vitality of the East Greek intellectual world in the mid and late fifth century may do much to explain the vitality of the *Histories*, and the enormous gap, not to mention the difference in style, between Hecataeus' works and Herodotus'.[3]

Thomas argues that even after the fall of Ionia, a lively intellectual scene remained in East Greece, and this context gave rise to Herodotus and Hippocrates. This means that Ionian tradition persisted in its southern regions. Why, though, did not Herodotus himself seem to be aware of this? When Herodotus was living in Halicarnassus, south of Ionia, many Ionian cities were already under Persian rule, and subject to the government of tyrants. These tyrants then were on the verge of invading Herodotus's Halicarnassus and Hippocrates's island of Kos. In this period, it was no longer an honor to be Ionian. This must be why Herodotus did not express much admiration of Ionian tradition. Still, there can be no doubt that he and Hippocrates inherited the Ionian spirit, even if unaware. Hence I would like to consider these two in connection to the earlier tradition of Ionian natural philosophy.

HIPPOCRATES

Until Hippocrates's time (480–377 BCE), epilepsy had been known in Egypt and Mesopotamia as the "divine affliction" caused by the gods or evil spirits. However, Hippocrates understood epilepsy to be due to natural causes, like any other disease. We can trace here the attitude of Ionian philosophy, which took the genesis of the world, heretofore explained as divine creation, to be explainable as the workings of nature (physis). The Ionians, exemplified by Thales, imported astronomy and mathematics from Egypt and Babylonia, but rejected astrology. When Hippocrates rejects the concept of divine affliction in considering epilepsy, he inherits that attitude:

> It is thus with regard to the disease called Divine Affliction: it appears to me to be nowise more divine nor more sacred than other diseases, but has a natural cause from which it originates like other affections. Men regard its nature and cause as divine from ignorance and wonder, because it is not at all like other diseases. And this notion of its divinity is kept up by their inability to comprehend it, and the simplicity of the mode by which it is cured, for men are freed from it by purifications and incantations. . . .
>
> They who first referred this malady to the gods appear to me to have been just such persons as the conjurors, purificators, mountebanks, and charlatans now are, who give themselves out for being excessively religious, and as knowing more than other people. Such persons, then, using the divinity as a pretext and screen of their own inability to afford any assistance, have given out that the disease is sacred. . . . And yet it would appear to me that their discourse savors not of piety, as they suppose, but rather of impiety, and as if there were no gods, and that what they hold to be holy and divine, were impious and unholy.[4]

Hippocrates rejected the gods as an explanation for disease. This was not, however, a denial of the gods per se. He rather rejected the magical form of religion, or a magic-based idea of the gods. Hippocrates's attitude is one peculiar to the Ionian natural philosophers. He tried to explain epilepsy as dysfunction of the brain and took the occasion to attack the position that it originated in the diaphragm as follows: "But the diaphragm has obtained its name [φρενες] from accident and usage [nomos], and not from reality or nature [physis]."[5] For the natural philosophers, the gods only manifest themselves through the working of physis, and medicine was a form of investigation of those workings. On the other hand, the gods as represented by humans were only a culturally constructed nomos.

In this connection, even today, Hippocrates is taken as the model for medicine not for his theory of disease, but for his ethics toward the patient. He treated poor patients for free. The Hippocratic Oath states, for example, "Whatever household I may have cause to visit I shall, distinguishing neither freeman nor slave, bring about no injustice within the house, and administer my treatment without prejudice." Again, "Any secrets I may discern of the household, whether related to medicine or not, I will hold tight and not divulge."

Where does this kind of attitude come from? Certainly not from Egypt or Mesopotamia. Athens, on the other hand, is just as unlikely. There was a keen interest in the arts and crafts (*techne*) in Ionia, and they were correspondingly well developed. Athens, though, lacked this. There the love of wisdom (*philo-sophia*) was held in high esteem; however, the practical arts were held in contempt as the work of slaves or the lower classes. By contrast, for Hippocrates, "Wherever the art of Medicine is loved, there is also a love of Humanity." This love of a fellow human is different from the Athenian love of wisdom (philosophy). The Athenian philosophers lacked love of techne. This was because they did not have sufficient love of humanity.

The love of humanity in Ionia is inseparable from the attitude of approaching humans, not through nomos, but through physis, an attitude that inevitably brackets distinction of human beings based on polis, tribe, clan, and status. And the source of this attitude was isonomia. Isonomia, or no-rule, does not simply place people on an equal footing in terms of political participation. It means more fundamentally the absence of the ruler and ruled hierarchy in the relations of production. Naturally, there is no recognition of the systems of slavery and bonded labor, as these simply run counter to nature or physis.

Hippocrates's attitude could not have come from Athenian democracy, based as it was in the slave system and the contempt and exclusion of foreigners. This is why it is wildly off the mark to claim that Ionian natural science did not pose ethical questions. Quite the contrary, it was the Ionians who opened up a path to the investigation of humanity and ethics. Even after the fall of the Ionian cities, this lineage spread through what we may call their diaspora. For example, the fifth-century BCE physician Alcmaeon explained sickness as a collapse of the internal isonomia, and its cause the emergence of a tyranny inside the body. This example indicates that natural philosophy was at the same time political philosophy: "The equality [isonomia] of the opposing powers which make up the body (e.g., the wet, the dry, the hot, the cold, the sweet, the bitter etc.) preserve health, whereas the monarchy of any one of them produces disease. As to why this is the case, the dictatorial right of any one side of an issue brings about collapse."[6]

The so-called Sophists too, in Athens, were mostly in the tradition of Ionian natural philosophy. While casting doubt on senses of legal justice that vary from culture to culture (nomos), they sought the basis of justice in a physis or natural law that underlay all of these. Based on this idea of natural law, the fourth-century BCE Sophist Alcidamas claimed, "The gods set the myriad of people free; nature has made no one a slave."[7]

Aristotle must have been well acquainted with the Sophists' arguments about natural law. In fact, the reason we are currently aware of the words of Alcidamas is that Aristotle quoted them. Further, Socrates's pupil Antisthenes asserted that the distinction between free man and slave, and the prejudice between man and woman, were rooted in nomos, hence must be set aside if one follows physis. It is highly likely that this line of thought was inherited from Socrates himself, as Plato and Aristotle must have been well aware. Nevertheless, Aristotle concludes, "It is clear [from the above], then, that some men are by nature [physis] free, and others are by nature slaves, and that for these latter slavery is both expedient and right."[8] In the *Republic*, Plato embraces a similar line of thought. This exemplifies the ethics of the Athenian philosophers.

·····················

HERODOTUS

Hippocrates has remained the standard in medical ethics to the present day. By contrast, it has only been relatively recently that Herodotus's historiography has come to be appreciated. Since Herodotus's time, the reputation of his *Histories* has suffered from comparison with the Athenian Thucydides's *History of the Peloponnesian War*. Thucydides himself was critical toward Herodotus.[9] Herodotus's *Histories* were thought to have incorporated many legends and fables, hence not to be objective records. Herodotus had been understood for that reason to be a fabulist, or a liar. However, the *Histories* receive a good deal of attention today as a repository of episodes and observations that can provide a clue for advancing interdisciplinary research into history.

The *Histories* tell the story of the Persian War. In fact, though, before beginning the record of the war proper, the work gives lengthy studies of the Persians, Egyptians, and many other peoples. This part of the work adduces lists, surveys, and analyses of natural factors from climate and geography to plants and animals, to institutions, to manners and customs. Naturally, the legends and traditions of these peoples are included among the material. In this sense, etymologically speaking, the title *Histories* serves as the literal description of its content: multiple narratives. History is typically understood to be about events and incidents. These words indicate phenomena where points of transition are particularly visible. However, there are phenomena where transformation is not apparent over the short term, but only becomes pronounced on the scale of hundreds, thousands, or even tens of thousands of years. These have not typically been understood to fall into the category of events. What Herodotus sought to relate at the same time as the incident of the Persian War were these kinds of events.

From antiquity, history has centered on political incidents and the rise and fall of states, that is to say, observation of incidents at the level where short-term transformation is evident. Thucydides recounts the Peloponnesian War from that perspective. This kind of historical description is not limited to Greece; we see the same thing in Chinese chronicles. It was Marx, and historians who came after, who began to cast doubt on such a historical perspective. Marx concentrated his attention on the type of incidents, such as transformation in modes of production, that become visible only when a long-term perspective is taken, while later the Annales School began to treat of incidents that required an even longer time scale to become visible, which they called the *longue durée* or "long term." Looking back from this perspective, it becomes clear that Herodotus, in the *Histories*, captured events at multiple timescales.

This is not the only reason why Herodotus's *Histories* remain paradigmatic even today. Even more relevant is the lack of ethnocentrism in his work. With the exception of a few prescient forerunners, it is really only since the 1970s that contemporary history and anthropology have been able to divest themselves of an ethnocentrism, or else a Eurocentrism.

Ethnocentrism has been the common state of affairs since antiquity. For example, the Greeks called anyone who did not speak the Greek language barbarians, and this is no special case. The Chinese not only called the non-Han peoples barbarians, but distinguished them according to direction, specifying the eastern, southern, western, and northern barbarians (*dongyi-nanman-xirong-beidi*). The Japanese were regarded as the eastern barbarians, while the Japanese themselves applied the same term to the unassimilated peoples to the geographical north in the Japanese islands.

Herodotus wrote archly of this kind of ethnocentrism. "The Egyptians call by the name of barbarians all such as speak a language different from their own."[10] Again, "[not only Dionysus], but almost all the names of the gods came into Greece from Egypt. My inquiries prove that they were all derived from a foreign source, and my opinion is that Egypt furnished the greater number."[11] Of course, contemporary Greeks held no such opinion. It was undoubtedly quite dangerous to make this kind of statement in Athens.

If so, how is it that Herodotus was able to escape this kind of ethnocentrism, that is to say, Grecocentrism? This is less a matter of his particular individual character, but comes rather from the Ionian environment. For example, Aristotle writes as follows:

> Those who live in a cold climate and in Europe are full of spirit, but wanting in intelligence and skill; and therefore they retain comparative freedom, but have no political organization, and are incapable of ruling over others. Whereas the natives of Asia are intelligent and inventive, but they are wanting in spirit, and therefore they are always in a state of subjection and slavery. But the [Greek] race, which is situated between them, is likewise intermediate in character, being high-spirited and also intelligent. Hence it continues free, and is the best-governed of any nation, and, if it could be formed into one state, would be able to rule the world.[12]

Here, "those who live in Europe" refers to nomadic society, whereas "natives of Asia" refers to Egypt, Persia, and other patrimonial bureaucratic states. The Greek people who occupy the middle way, then, transcend both, and consequently are fit to rule them. This is prototypical Grecocentrism, or better Athenocentrism. But in Ionia, a multiethnic cluster of colonies situated in Asia Minor, this kind of ethnocentrism could not possibly sink roots. The Ionians were Greek at the same time they were Asian, while at the same time being neither. The Ionian natural philosophers were each affiliated with their own polis; however, they lived essentially in the cosmopolis. Herodotus was raised to the south of Ionia after their cities had already fallen to the Persians, and despite it being the time of Athenian zenith, somehow retained the lineage of Ionian thought.

One can cite as a forerunner of Herodotus Hecataeus of Miletus (550–476 BCE). He rejected Homeric verse history, and, distinguishing legend from fact, sought to write history in prose. It is clear that Herodotus's works are an extension of this thinking. However, the Ionian legacy he inherited could not limit its account to history in the narrow sense, that is to say, a recitation of political incidents. As outlined before, the natural philosophers beginning with Anaximander did not simply inquire into external nature. They sought to capture the history of living organisms and human society in its entirety as a natural history. Geography would be one link in this chain. Hecataeus's *Travels around the Earth* (*Periegesis*) is a book of geographical history. What Herodotus inherited is this natural philosophical attitude that sees events as fundamentally part of a natural history.

The *Histories* of Herodotus are an effort to interpret nomos from the perspective of physis. Herodotus subjected any given incident to ceaselessly inquiry (*elenchos*), as to whether it was a matter of nomos, of physis, or a combination of the two. Here, he regards nomos (culture, institutions) as historical and relative phenomena, and seeks the basis in physis, the universal principle underlying the transformations of nomos. This was his method of survey and analysis of the manners and customs of various regions. As Rosalind Thomas argues, Herodotus shows a basic sympathy with Hippocrates, who poses the question of how natural environment can affect human character and behavior, in the section "On Air, Water, and Place" in *On Ancient Medicine*.

Let us take another illustration of Herodotus's antipathy to Grecocentrism. Here, he introduces a discussion that occurred among the ruling elite of Persia. Otanes, one of the seven conspirators, advocates the adoption of democracy:

> A king, besides, is beyond all other men inconsistent with himself. . . . [He] sets aside the laws of the land, puts men to death without trial, and subjects the women to violence. The rule of the many, on the other hand, has, in the first place, the fairest of names, to wit, *isonomia*; and further it is free from all those outrages which a king is wont to commit. There, places are given by lot, the magistrate is answerable for what he does, and measures rest with the commonalty. I vote, therefore, that we do away with monarchy, and raise the people to power. For the people are all in all.[13]

In response, Megabyzus extols the virtues of oligarchy, followed by Darius, who asserts the superiority of monarchy. In the end, Darius's opinion carries the day, and, as a result, he was crowned king (Darius I of the Achaemenid Empire).

This discussion of the political body anticipates Aristotle's observations in *Politics*, written when Athens was in decline. However, is it likely that such a debate could really have occurred among the Persians? Herodotus himself obviously anticipated this doubt and offered the following explanation: "In the course of [Mardonius's] voyage along the coast of Asia he came to Ionia; and here I have a marvel to relate which will greatly surprise those Greeks who cannot believe that Otanes advised the seven conspirators to make Persia a commonwealth. Mardonius put down all the despots throughout Ionia, and in lieu of them established democracies."[14] To clarify, it was the Persian, Mardonius, who dismantled the tyrannies by which the Ionian cities had till then been governed and reorganized them as democracies. Herodotus obviously speaks ironically in order to challenge ideas entrenched in Athens at the time, still current today, that Greece is democratic while Persia is despotic.

<hr />

HOMER

It is clear enough that Ionian natural philosophy began as a critique of religion, in that it sought to explain the world without reference to the gods. However, such an attitude did not appear out of nowhere in the middle of the sixth century BCE. It was nurtured throughout the seventh century by the rapid development of commerce and trade among the colonies centering on Miletus and the quickening pace of overseas settlement. Further, there were cultural developments peculiar to Ionia that came before, in particular the poetic works of Homer in the mid-eighth century, and Hesiod around the turn of the eighth century BCE. Both expressed themselves in the Ionian dialect and were recorded in script developed in Ionia. Their work later spread to the Greek mainland and became known as the fount and common source of Greek civilization.

The works of Homer and Hesiod should be seen as rooted in the earlier Greek legends and oral tradition, rather than as imaginative works. However, the materials on which they were believed to base their work do not survive. Thus, presumably the Greeks after them learned their legends from Homer and Hesiod. Seen this way, one could say that the

Olympian gods were indeed their creations. But, from another stand-point, their own experience of Ionian society was projected in their works.

The first point to note in this respect about the Olympian gods is that they no longer retain the characteristics of the gods of a tribal society. For the Ionian colonists, who retained no tie with their place of origin, the Olympian gods were essential to align and solidify to form a polis. Mere extension of the tribal deities could not have served this purpose. Perhaps, as Herodotus presumed, the Olympian gods were introduced from Asia. Yet this type of god did not survive in Asia itself. In Asia, the character of the gods changed along with formation of empire, becoming a world deity to match the scale of world empire. In Egypt and Mesopotamia we see the advent of monotheism and the idea of a god that is the creator of the world. As Weber points out, the idea of a creator god finds its source in the fundamental transformation of the natural world we see in large-scale agriculture by irrigation. This concept of a sole creator deity did not fit the Greek situation where poleis of every sort coexisted side by side, and agriculture still relied on natural rainfall. Meanwhile, the Olympian gods found easy acceptance. Each Greek polis found an Olympian deity to worship in place of the deities of their origin.

The gods of Olympus were indispensable for securing solidarity among the Greek poleis, a point discerned most straightforwardly in the Olympic festival that venerated Zeus as the supreme god. However, the weak point of the nonnative Olympian gods was an inability to sink roots deep within the polis or to the level of the individual. They were from the start removed from the communal basis of the tribes. Hence, once a critical eye was cast on them, rootless as they were they could only withdraw into the heavens. Of course, this occurred gradually and not at a stroke.

We can locate the beginning of the destruction of the gods in the poetry of Homer. On first reading, all one finds in Homer is the ceaseless activities of the personified gods. However, this personification itself is the first step toward their destruction. This concept of the gods appears primitive but is not. In a primitive conception, the gods appear without personality as a supernatural and undefinable power. However, once the gods are personified, what was once supernatural is placed on the plane of the natural world. The gods are superior in degree to human beings, but belong to the same natural dimension. They respond to the same feelings and desires as humans, and find themselves enmeshed in self-limiting struggle. Zeus is worshipped as the sovereign deity, but does not possess the power to suppress other gods. Likewise, gods occupy the stage in Homer but are afforded virtually no reverence. The gods are the same violent, capricious, and irresponsible characters as the human rulers.

In *The Iliad*, the origins of the Trojan War and the course it took are ascribed almost entirely to this kind of struggle among the gods. However, the gods are not really in control. For example, in the battle between Hector and Achilles, the gods each choose sides, but cannot guarantee a conclusion. In heaven, Zeus weighs their fates in a golden balance. And according to this, Hector must die. In other words, the gods cannot intervene in human destiny. In the opening of *The Odyssey*, Zeus speaks as follows: "See now, how men lay blame upon us gods for what is after all nothing but their own folly. [They say the whirlwind is by our doing, but through their own unrighteous actions, they contravene the judgment of the fates, and invite these catastrophes on themselves]."[15]

What Homer reveals here is not just the idea that humans are subject to the whims of something beyond their comprehension, but that the gods are subject to the same. Humans are in unceasing conflict. The gods, too, are in unceasing conflict. What could be subjecting both gods and humans to such a fate? In a word, it is an antagonistic form of reciprocity. This leads to an escalating series of blood exchanges. The Olympian gods are unable to restrain it, because they themselves are put in motion by this chain. Both *The Iliad* and *The Odyssey* share as a theme this principle of an ungovernable reciprocity that is finally, in the end, overcome. The question Homer poses, whether in respect to humans or gods, is what is the real nature, or physis, of the forces to which they are subjected? Ionian philosophy is a radical form of such inquiry.

The view that the Homeric poems were composed by a single author was early subject to scholarly doubt. The generally recognized position today is that there was a historical person named Homer active in the mid-eighth century BCE, who took memories stored by bardic poets from the Heroic Age and put them into contemporary verse form. However, this bears scrutiny itself. What is represented in the Homeric epics is the Heroic Age, that is to say, a society where the strata of the nobility formed a council, and the community at large, kings, nobility, and common members included, constituted a popular assembly. However, the Trojan War is usually located at the end of the Mycenaean period (ca. 1200 BCE), which implies a highly developed Bronze Age civilization under an Asiatic state with a patrimonial bureaucratic system. It follows that the Heroic Age depicted by Homer did not exist at the time of the events, and one cannot transmit something that has never existed.

The important thing in approaching the Homeric epics is not the question of authorship, but rather for whom it was intended. And this would of course initially have been the contemporary citizenry of Ionia. One cannot understand the Homeric epics outside of this context. In the dark ages after the fall of the Mycenaean civilization, city-states sprang up all over Greece, some ruled by kings and some by the nobility, and engaged in ceaseless conflict. This was the state of affairs present to Homer and his readers. In that sense, the heroic age depicted in Homer does not represent the following age, but a projection of contemporary social reality in the Greek city-states onto the past. This is why, at the same time the Homeric epics celebrate the martial exploits of heroes in battle, they express an intense antipathy to war. For example, one finds throughout *The Iliad* the voices of women, raised in lamentation and cries of anger toward war.

The Homeric epics share no ground with the ideology that glorifies the heroes of the warrior or aristocratic classes, and contain within them a critique of the endless warfare between the polis and the clans. At the end of *The Iliad*, when Achilles has killed Hector, he renounces any further retribution. By the time of *The Odyssey*, then, there really are no heroes. Odysseus wanders the land as a mere foreigner and returns home a beggar. He does indeed exact revenge on the suitors who tormented his family in his absence but renounces escalation of this to their families. Both *The Iliad* and *The Odyssey* end by rejecting the infinite chain of vendettas.

From the point of view of modes of exchange, personal warfare and vengeance are expressions of an antagonistic reciprocity (a form of mode of exchange A). Within city-states formed through a compact of multiple tribes, this is kept under control. However, among the ruling strata personal combat and struggles against other city-states continue unabated. In this sense, antagonistic reciprocity remains. What brings an end to these conflicts is the unification of multiple city-states under a patrimonial bureaucratic state after passing through this process of struggle. In other words, reciprocity of violence (mode A) is overcome by a social contract between ruler and ruled (mode B).

The despotic state (a patrimonial bureaucratic system) constructed a system with a bureaucracy and standing army that are not dependent on reciprocal human relations. This is where the rule of law emerges, which is fully realized when the ruler (king) becomes bound by the laws he himself has promulgated. This kind of rule of law removes the principle of antagonistic reciprocity at a stroke, as exemplified by the code of Hammurabi and its famous provision of "an eye for an eye." This is not an exhortation to revenge. Far from it; it is rather a means for prohibiting its escalation.

As mentioned before, the Mycenaean state in Greece was a patrimonial bureaucratic state. In the dark ages after its fall, there again appeared constant strife between tribes and city-states. However, the city-states in the Greek lands did not at this time repeat the path to a despotic state. How then were the Greeks able to abolish this antagonistic reciprocity while avoiding the path to despotism? The key to this process lay in the colonial cities of Ionia, where a social contract among equals was born among the colonists drawn from various clans and poleis. Homer and his audience must have been living in the time when this principle of the polis was being established. Hirono Seki describes Achilles's renunciation of retribution in *The Iliad* as follows:

> What could possibly end the escalation of this vicious circle of violence? Homer's answer is already hinted at in the representation on the shield that the goddess Thetis gives to her son Achilles amid lamentations over his return to battle. On the face of the shield, scenes of beauty and abundance are carved in sharp contrast to the calamity and misfortune of war. In the center of this peaceful world are the figures of citizens conducting a trial in the public square. This trial, conducted by citizens' assembly, is diametrically opposed to the assembly of the Achaean army, where a soldier is struck by Odysseus's mace when he urges withdrawal from Troy. By judgment by debate and reason, the unreasonable judgment of Zeus's golden balance becomes useless. Versus judgment by blind force, which only worsens the situation, the vital force of speech ascends the stage, guiding people to fellowship and peace.[16]

What is important to note here is that, in the mid-eighth century BCE when Homer wrote, the place where one might actually witness "the figures of citizens listening to a trial in the public square" was in fact not Greek cities in general, but rather only in the cities of Ionia. In Ionia, the law is not something handed down by kings or gods. It is rather built from consensus among equal citizens. This process demands debate and common inquiry. Homer either takes the isonomia that he experiences in Ionia as a premise or foresees it.

What should be clear from the above is that Homer's personification of the gods is not mythological in nature. It rather lays bare the mechanism driving humans, and finds the means of overcoming it in assembly and trial in the public square. In this sense, we may say that Homer anticipates the critique of religion in Ionian natural philosophy.

HESIOD

Hesiod is a poet and a thinker who follows Homer and is conscious of his works. In *Theogony*, he organizes the creation myth as follows. In the beginning was Chaos. From Chaos was born Gaia (earth), Tartaros (the underworld), and Eros (love). From Gaia was born Uranus (the heavens) and Pontos (the sea). These gods are the deification of nature, not its personification. The first truly personified gods are born of the union of Gaia and Uranus, and give rise to the Titan race. When Gaia is betrayed by Uranus, she plots with her youngest child, Kronos, to take revenge. Kronos marries his elder sister Rhea, but because of a presentiment that he would be overthrown just as he had overthrown his own father, he swallows the children of their union, Hestia, Hades, Demeter, Poseidon, and Hera, as soon as they are born. Rhea, however, schemes to hide and save the sixth child, Zeus. When Zeus comes of age, he forces his father to disgorge his older siblings and leads them to live on Mount Olympus. This Olympian race of gods lived in constant struggle with the Titans. Zeus finally prevails over the Titans and becomes the sovereign of the gods in place of his father Kronos. The three brothers, Zeus, Poseidon, and Hades, choose their domains by lot, Zeus over the skies, Poseidon over the seas, and Hades over the underworld.

This type of myth is found over the Asian region as a whole. Generally speaking, it reflects the process by which the struggle among independent city-states leads to the formation of a patrimonial bureaucratic state. Just as the victor of these struggles is raised to the position of a king, in these myths, the god who seizes hegemony is raised to a position of transcendence. However, Hesiod's organization of the Greek legends differs in the following way from regions in which a despotic state was established. Certainly, Zeus is depicted ascending to hegemony, reflecting the process whereby a new order is established out of the dark ages of the struggle among the poleis. But the order here established is not that of a despotic empire but rather a federation of multiple poleis. The elevation of Zeus to the supreme position among the gods reflects this, symbolized more than anywhere else in the opening of the Olympic Games to honor him (776 BCE).

Nonetheless, the idea of a transcendental God did not arise in Greece. God in Mesopotamia and Egypt was the supreme creator. As discussed earlier, this concept of God finds its root in the radical transformation of the natural world enabled by large-scale irrigation-based agriculture, and its organization by the despotic state. However, this idea could not take root in Greece, where agriculture relied on the accidents of rain. Zeus has a transcendental aspect in regard to humans and the other gods; however, he was subordinate to nature or its embodiment in the gods.

For example, Kronos (time) and Eros rule over Zeus. Gaia as well holds a superior position as something more fundamental. That is to say, Zeus, a deification of the human, is subordinate to the gods as deification of nature. In short, Hesiod places personified gods in a position inferior to the power of the natural world. As it happens, the natural philosophers later rejected the gods of Hesiod but inherited his framework of thinking.

After narrating this natural historical genesis, the *Theogony* turns to the creation of human society. This explanation has a basis in mythology but, in fact, looks at the history of human society in terms of fire (technology) and labor. This begins with Prometheus and the theft of fire, and its gift to human society. In response, Zeus metes out a punishment to humans in the form of Pandora. "For of old the tribes of men lived on the earth apart from evil, and grievous toil, and sore diseases that bring the fates of death to men. But in these days of evil men speedily wax old. For the woman [Pandora] took off the great lid of the Jar with her hands, and made a scattering thereof, and devised baleful sorrows for men. Only Hope abode within, in her unbreakable chamber under the lips of the Jar, and flew not forth."[17]

From that point begins a life of cruel labor. However, hope remains. This narrative of paradise lost and regained was not exceptional, but rather a commonplace in Mesopotamia. The Hebrew myth of the Garden of Eden is one variation. What is conspicuous about Hesiod's thinking in this case, however, is that he saw it in terms of development of historical stages. Though couched in the language of myth, in fact he places technology at the cornerstone of this narrative, such that within it resides the relation of humans and nature at the foundation of history.

In Hesiod's way of thinking, there formerly was a golden age (or golden race of superior mortal men), succeeded by a far inferior silver race, and a violent and warlike Bronze Age. After the subsequent Heroic Age, then, follows the dismal misery of the Iron Age. Here, gold and silver are symbolic, but bronze and iron are meant literally as the stage of civilization based on bronze and iron implements. The Heroic Age is represented by the time of the Trojan War. The Iron Age indicates the period of enormous and powerful state formation enabled by iron weapons. This is the age in which Hesiod lived, and the period that sees the emergence of despotic states with the tribute system.

The Iron Age, that is to say, the present age of conflict, is a terrible, wretched state of affairs. "Neither by day shall they ever cease from weariness and woe, nor in the night from wasting, and sore cares shall the gods give them. Howbeit even for them shall good be mingled with evil."[18] However, there is hope in this age of misery, the prescription for which Hesiod specifies: "Lay thou these things to heart, and hearken to justice and utterly forget violence."[19] Hesiod calls for his readers to believe in the justice of the gods and apply themselves to labor. "By works do men wax rich in flocks and gear: yea, and by work shalt thou be far dearer to immortals and to mortals. . . . Work is no reproach: the reproach is idleness."[20]

Hesiod finds hope not over the horizon in some other world, but in the application of labor in the present world. We would never expect this kind of thinking to emerge in a society where warriors rule and labor is left to slaves and serfs. This is the worldview of colonists in the Ionian provinces. To put it in Weber's terms, this is the work ethic of the farmers who cultivate their own lands. The people of Ionia certainly had this ethos in common.

Thales and the natural philosophers would not appear till much later; however, the ground was prepared for their emergence here in the eighth century. In contrast to the Athenians, the Ionians placed great emphasis on technology. According to George Thomson, "The two centuries preceding the Persian War saw the adoption of the sheep-shears, rotary quern, wine press, and crane. After them, no further inventions are recorded before the Hellenistic age. Thus, in industrial as well as commercial progress, the fifth century was a turning point. What was it that brought the movement to a stop? The answer is that this was the century in which 'slavery seized on production in earnest.'"[21]

Rather than "slavery seizing on production," though, it is precisely the contempt for labor (manual work) in Athens that led to the system of slavery. This scorn for manual labor is not, of course, peculiar to Athens. As we saw earlier in Herodotus, contempt for manual work is generally characteristic of nomadic and warlike peoples, to say nothing of the great patriarchal, bureaucratic states or slave-dependent societies. Consequently, in the ancient world, a society that affirms the value of labor and technology was a rarity. Ionia may very well be the sole example. If one locates, as Weber does, the source of the work ethic that sustains modern capitalism in religious form, behind the development of commerce and trade in Ionia we may indeed find a species of "religious transformation."[22]

The Ionians actively affirmed the value of labor, as we see in Hesiod. In that sense, Ionia was a society of practice. Aristotle states that a certain leisure is required for scholarship to flourish:

> But as more arts were invented, and some were directed to the necessities of life, others to recreation, the inventors of the latter were naturally always regarded as wiser than the inventors of the former, because their branches of knowledge did not aim at utility. Hence when all such inventions were already established, the sciences which do not aim at giving pleasure or at the necessities of life were discovered, and first in the places where men first began to have leisure. This is why the mathematical arts were founded in Egypt; for there the priestly caste was allowed to be at leisure.[23]

For Aristotle, the contemplative arts or *theoria* are superior, and leisure or *schole* is their prerequisite.

In Ionia, though, even if the people attained some degree of leisure, their life did not then become contemplative. In Asia, the contemplative or theoretical arts were advanced by the priesthood. In both Mesopotamia and Egypt, the concept of a transcendental God was established along with the patrimonial bureaucratic state. The priests who were in charge of religion also advanced inquiries into nature, such as astronomy, mathematics, and so forth. In Ionia, there was no ruler or bureaucracy, nor the idea of a transcendental God. Though there were ritual specialists and priests, they held neither power nor authority. In a society of isonomia, there is no recognition of a transcendental position.

Ionia did not have a class of people (priest or nobility) in a privileged relation to leisure. Thales, for example, fulfilled a variety of roles, from engineer to politician. Their knowledge was always practical. For example, while the Ionians were receptive to astronomy from the Asian states, they did not accept astrology, and while they absorbed the gods of Asia, they did not accept the concept of a transcendental God. This is the kind of mind-set that preceded the birth of natural philosophy.

I would make an additional note on the difference between the Ionian poleis and the poleis on the Greek mainland. The Greek polis was a covenant community formed by embracing a new god in place of the tribal gods of their origin. This new set of deities constituted the pantheon of Olympus. For example, in Ionia Apollo was the guardian deity, while in Athens it was Athena. However, the difference between the Greek and Ionian poleis lay not in the gods they worship, but rather in the attitude toward the gods and priesthood. In the Ionian poleis, composed of settlers from other places, the gods were a ritual symbolization of the social contract among individuals who had broken from the old tribal collectives. Because of this, the priestly caste had no special authority. By contrast, in the poleis on the Greek mainland, the gods and the priestly caste were an extension of the old tribal authority. So, for example, the oracle at Delphi held authority. In this sense, the philosophers of Athens had a great deal more of the priestly caste than the thinkers in Ionia.

Conversely, the thinkers of Ionia had a standpoint that went beyond the narrow collective as far back as Hesiod's time. For example, Hesiod's idea of justice transcended the confines of a single nation: "But whoever deals straight judgment to stranger and townsmen alike, and no whit departs from justice, their city flourishes and the people prosper therein. And there is in their land peace, and nursing of children, and Zeus doth never decree war for them. Neither does Famine ever visit men who deal straight judgments, nor Doom, but with delight they tend the works that are their care."[24]

Justice of the polis must be something universal. That is to say, the principle that enables the formation of the polis must be applicable to the cosmopolis. Consequently, the truly just state is only fully realizable in the "perpetual peace" among states (Kant). This view is quintessentially Ionian. The natural philosophers emerged through the rejection of the myths of Hesiod. However, the core of Ionian philosophy already resided in his thought.

Chapter 3

The Essential Points of
Ionian Natural Philosophy

THE CRITIQUE OF RELIGION

The natural philosophers beginning with Thales sought an explanation of the world without reference to the gods. This did not necessarily imply a rejection of gods per se. It did, however, imply clearing the scene of the personified gods of Olympus. However, all this ferment did not appear suddenly in mid-sixth-century Ionia. We can trace its beginning back to Hesiod's time. As outlined before, Ionian characteristics appear in his *Theogony*. More specifically, this tale, mythological in one aspect, shows an aspect of rationalism (a form of deism) in another. However, there is one point on which the later natural philosophy departs decisively from Hesiod.

The accepted interpretation regarding the emergence of natural philosophy is that, in the cities of Ionia, where commerce and the trades had advanced to a high degree, people began to think in rational terms without relying on myths or magical arts. But if this was true, natural philosophy could have arisen at the zenith of Ionian prosperity in the seventh century BCE. But natural philosophy appeared amid the fall of Ionian cities during the sixth century BCE. That is to say, it emerged at a time of crisis.

This crisis is typically identified with the invasions by Lydia and Persia. In fact, the Ionian cities were first conquered by Lydia and placed under the rule of tyrants tied to the Lydian state. However, the cause of the invasion was not simply external. There had to be a prior internal crisis. As an example, Thales's attempt to persuade the Ionian cities to organize a federation in response to the external threat was frustrated due to the lack of consensus. This indicates that the crisis rather resided within. Gaps between rich and poor, and ruler–ruled relations, were becoming prominent internal features in different Ionian poleis by this time. This signaled the breakdown of isonomia. As a means of naturalizing these relations, the idea of a community based on tribal or mythical affiliation began to be emphasized over the idea of the polis as a collective based on social contract.

It was in order to counter such a climate that Thales and the natural philosophers of Miletus offered an explanation of the world without reference to the gods. It was their way of reconfirming the identity of the polis, not in tribal or mythological lineage, but in a social contract. This was linked to the strategy to rebuild a society without the ruler–ruled relation, which is to say, reestablishing isonomia. Natural philosophy is, in this sense, fundamentally social philosophy.

Prior to this, Ionians did not think about the meaning of their social practice. As a rule, people become aware of the significance of something only when it is disappearing. For the Ionians this would be in the middle of the sixth century. In the various regions of Ionia, as the relations of isonomia progressively deteriorated, democratic reforms were initiated. In most cases these resulted in tyranny. In Samos, for example, reforms initiated by Polycrates and his confidante Pythagoras ended in him assuming the position of tyrant in 538 BCE. Polycrates's plan was to bring about political reform. However, through this process he gradually turned dictatorial. Behind this process, though, were social realities in need of reform, and the tyranny received the support of the people. We have to assume this sort of situation played out not only in the island of Samos but in the entire territory of Ionia. The natural philosophers' inquiry into the primal substance, or arche, originated in this context. Thales's young associate Anaximander writes as follows: "From [such] things existing objects come to be, into them too does their destruction take place, according to what must be: for they give recompense and pay restitution to each other for their injustice according to the ordering of time."[1]

There is a dissonance in applying words such as *recompense* and *restitution* to nature. However, if we take his words as a statement of social philosophy, we can discern here a denunciation of tyranny and class, and a call for restitution of isonomia.

According to Aristotle, Thales took water to be the arche (original substance). Here is Aristotle's summary from *The Metaphysics*:

> Thales, the founder of this type of philosophy, says the principle is water (for which reason he declared that the earth rests on water), getting the notion perhaps from seeing that the nutriment of all things is moist, and that heat itself is generated from the moist and kept alive by it (and that from which they come to be is a principle of all things). He got his notion from this fact, and from the fact that the seeds of all things have a moist nature, and that water is the origin of the nature of moist things.
>
> Some think that even the ancients who lived long before the present generation, and first framed accounts of the gods, had a similar view of nature; for they made Okeanos and Tethys the parents of creation, and described the oath of the gods as being by water, to which [poets gave] the name of Styx; for what is oldest is most honourable, and the most honourable thing is that by which one swears.[2]

As Aristotle hints, not just for Thales, but for the other natural philosophers too, arche seems to be based on a Hesiod-like mythology rather than observation. For example, Thales' student Anaximander located arche in the apeiron (the unlimited or the boundless). The boundless in itself is a single element (*stoicheion*). However, through its motion, internally opposed things, such as hot and cold, or dry and moist, divide and are given rise, generating all things.

Anaximander's "the boundless" seems abstract in comparison with Thales's "water." However, this too is in a way another word for Hesiod's Chaos. For Hesiod, Chaos gives rise to Gaia (earth), and Tartaros (the nether world), which resides in its depths. From their union is born Uranus (the sky), the mountains, and Pontos (the sea). An identical set of relations is visible in Anaximander when water, air, and earth are born of the boundless.

However, what is crucial for natural philosophy is not the identity of arche (original substance) but rather that it moves of itself. Matter and motion here are inseparable. In the world of myth, the cause of matter's motion (i.e., change) is the gods. If one removes the gods from the system, one must seek the cause of motion in matter itself. For Thales, water is self-moved. There is no cause for the motion lying behind it. The original substance Thales identifies moves of itself. This has led to the view that it was something like a spirit or an anima. Thales himself is purported to have said, "All things are full of gods."[3] J. M. Cornford, in this respect, found in natural philosophers a hylozoism (the idea that all matter has life) and assumed it has its roots in primitive ways of thinking. However, Thales did not introduce a magical way of thinking. Quite the opposite; it was in order to move away from magical thinking that he conceived the self-moving original substance.

To reiterate, the idea of a self-moving matter was a cornerstone of Io-nian natural philosophy, shared by all in its lineage. Where their thinking diverged was on the question of what this original matter might be. For Thales, it was water. Anaximander, on the other hand, while recognizing four composite factors (earth, water, fire, air), posited a substratum or *hypokeimenon*, because these four elements are mutually transmutable. This substratum was the boundless or apeiron. Put this way, Anaximander appears more profound than Thales, who simply identified arche as water.

However, Anaximander's pupil Anaximenes went on to locate the primordial matter in air.[4] Subsequently, Heraclitus found it in fire. This development seems rather strange in that all these things were already contained in Anaximander's four composite factors. If Anaximander had appeared after these thinkers as a synthesis, that would make sense. But why did these later thinkers feel the need to return to Thales?

Anaximander's boundless or infinite (apeiron) is not matter that can be known through the senses, but rather an abstract idea.[5] As I have explained, this was a restatement of the mythological idea of chaos, and not a decisive advance on Thales's thought. Hence, to really transcend mythology, it was necessary to once again assert that matter was moved not by the gods, but of itself. Thinkers from Anaximenes on pushed their thought in that direction.

What would happen, by contrast, if one denied the self-motion of mat-ter, that is to say, if one sees motion and matter as separate? In that case, one must posit an agent or subject to bring about motion. Here, though the gods are withdrawn, an idealistic agency is reintroduced. In Plato's thought, matter cannot move by itself. What effects this motion is God, that is to say, the demiurges that purposively arrange the universe. Aris-totle, on the other hand, in some sense accepted the position of natural philosophy, and recognized the self-motion of substance. However, he understood motion (becoming, or *werden*) to arise from causes immanent in matter. Aristotle does not introduce an agent such as the demiurges, but *cause* fulfills the same role.

Aristotle understood cause to come in four forms: material and efficient, final and formal. He posited that Thales and the Milesians had discovered material and efficient causes, but not formal and final causes. However, it is not that the Milesians failed to recognize these types of cause; they purposefully rejected them. Formal and final causes can only be found after a thing has come into being. From such a post-*factum* perspective, Aristotle arrived at the view that motion has a purpose (or an end). He called this the final cause or *telos*, which in fact is the projection of the endpoint onto the origin.

The Milesian school asserted the self-motion of matter as a way to reject positing something behind the motion, that is to say, the mythological thinking that posits the god as creator or demiurge. And yet, Aristotle's idea of final cause carries in it the gods banished by the Milesian school. Of course Aristotle did not reintroduce the gods as such; he rather discovered God as the ultimate cause of motion, the prime mover. Thereby his first philosophy (metaphysics) becomes a theology.[6] It is no wonder that Aristotle's first philosophy subsequently came to serve as the basis of Islamic and Christian theology.

After this kind of theology became dominant, the natural philosophy of the pre-Socratics from Thales to Democritus was pushed into oblivion. It would not be until the European Renaissance that they were reassessed. What broke the long dominance of Aristotelian speculation was the reintroduction of natural philosophy. The Renaissance literally was a rebirth of Ionian philosophy. Two factors enabled this rebirth: first, the preservation of Ionian natural philosophy in the Islamic world and, second, the rise in Europe, in particular in Italy, of a set of conditions similar to those that obtained among the Ionian city-states.

Ernst Bloch writes, "In the static worldview of the Middle Ages we see reflected a society that stood static, but for them, it is exactly the reverse. They held that the natural state of a body is to be at rest. They regarded motion as an anomaly; hence, any motion of bodies is consumed of itself, which is why a body runs more slowly if it has been in motion for a while. The anomalous impulse dissipates, and the body achieves its natural state of rest, and is finally satisfied."[7] By contrast, in the free cities of the Renaissance, the idea of movement and generation without a telos was easy to conceive. However, this did not continue for long, as the free cities were quickly absorbed into the state (absolute monarchy). Along with this process, the concept of self-moving matter too became untenable, and a new form of dualism (mind and extension in Descartes) became dominant.

It bears repeating that the idea of the self-motion of matter is the essential point in a natural philosophy. Giordano Bruno (1548–1600), condemned as a heretic and burned at the stake, was the first to grasp the significance of this as the *natura naturans* or nature that produces nature. Bloch comments as follows: "Poor matter, which is called gray and graceless, leaden, dead and dull, is reanimated by Giordano Bruno, in that he brings the pre-Socratic view as neo-pagan back into the world, and takes back from transcendence what it has stolen from matter."[8] Through Bruno, matter as self-generating nature was resurrected. Hence Bruno is subject even today to the same accusation as the Ionian thinkers in their day, that is to say, that he was a magical thinker who took matter to be animated.

Bruno's cosmology was also in line with natural philosophy. Bruno backed Copernicus in advocating a heliocentric hypothesis, overturning the Aristotelian/Ptolemaic system. However, at the same time he criticized Copernicus, arguing that the solar system is only one of multiple worlds in the infinite universe. In fact, though, Bruno is bringing back the ideas of Anaximander, who held that the universe was infinite and our world one of many. Though unaware himself, Bruno effected a renaissance or rebirth of Ionian philosophy.

It was Spinoza who comprehensively developed the idea of natura naturans (nature that produces nature) advanced by Bruno. In Spinoza's thought, self-producing Nature is God, whereas the personified God is only an imaginary projection modeled on one's family experience. In criticizing anthropomorphism, Spinoza playfully proposes that if a triangle could speak, it would say, in like manner, that God is eminently triangular, while a circle would say that the divine nature is eminently circular. Thus each would ascribe to God its own attributes, would assume itself to be like God, and look on everything else as ill-shaped.[9] Although Spinoza does not refer to the natural philosophers, this remark is nearly identical to that of the itinerant Ionian poet Xenophanes of Colophon (ca. 570–475 BCE):

But mortals think gods are begotten,
and have the clothing, voice, and body of mortals.
Now if cattle, horses, or lions had hands
and were able to draw with their hands and perform works like men,
horses like horses and cattle like cattle
would draw the forms of the gods, and make their bodies
just like the body [each of them] had.[10]

Xenophanes is reported to have continued, "One God, greatest among gods and men, not at all like to mortals in body nor in thought."[11] That is to say, while rejecting an anthropomorphic God, Xenophanes affirmed One God. This allows us to presume that natural philosophers had some sort of divinity or God in their mind when they rejected the gods. For them, however, this was something beyond representation. Consequently, the critique of idolatry needs to be discerned particularly as a distinctive characteristic of natural philosophy.

POIESIS AND BECOMING

Aristotle drew a distinction between the becoming of nature and the human activity of producing or making (*poiesis*). In his way of thinking, physics (or natural science) takes as its object something that itself has no producer, hence can be neither a productive matter (poiesis) nor a practical matter (*praxis*), but only theoretical.

> There is a science of nature, and evidently it must be different both from practical and from productive science. For in the case of productive science the principle of movement is in the producer and not in the product, and is either an art or some other faculty. And similarly in practical science the movement is not in the thing done, but rather in the doers. But the science of the natural philosopher deals with the things that have *in themselves* a principle of movement. It is clear from these facts, then, that natural science must be neither practical nor productive. [book II]
>
> Therefore, if all thought is either practical or productive or theoretical, physics must be a theoretical science, but it will theorize about such being as admits of being moved and about substance-as-defined for the most part only as not separable from matter. [book 6][12]

However, when Aristotle finds a telos or final cause in nature, in fact he is looking at nature from the perspective of the maker/God, and rendering this position interior to nature. Meanwhile, the Ionian philosophers refuse even the idea of a final cause. Nature's becoming of itself differs from making precisely because it has no cause or aim. However, to think of becoming in this way is in no way to deny the significance of making/production. Quite the opposite; the Ionian natural philosophers placed great importance on production and technology, and inquired into becoming based on this.

As noted before, there were many technological innovations in the period of Ionian ascendancy, but there were virtually none in the age of Athens. This difference corresponds to the difference between Ionian natural philosophers and Aristotle. Unlike Plato, Aristotle did seek to inherit Ionian natural philosophy; however, his emphasis was placed on its biological aspect. Aristotle's formal and final causes are modeled on the realization of biological forms latent in the embryo or seed. While this was useful in explaining the persistence over time of the same species, it provided no account of how a new species could come into being. More to the point, the problem seems never to have occurred to Aristotle.

The reason is simple. Aristotle understood by productive work (poiesis) poetics and agriculture. He shared the general Athenian contempt for manufacture and technology. For this reason, he was unable to see that agriculture is rooted in a kind of technology. For example, anyone involved in cultivation and domestication is more or less aware of breed improvement and generation of new species through it. Persons acquainted with this kind of experience are likely to reach the conclusion that the species extant in the world are variants of older species. Ionian theories of nature seem to be rooted in this kind of supposition. The realization that through the recombination and division of arche—whether it was water, air, or any other element—the variety of things in the world is generated, did not come from metaphysical speculation, but from a perception based on physical practice. This perception must have been rooted in the experience of technology that flourished in Ionia.

Benjamin Farrington observes the following with respect to Anaximander's cosmology: "This very arresting cosmology, while it has obvious reminiscences of the potter's yard, the smithy, or the kitchen, leaves no room for Marduk [the Babylonian creator deity] at all. Even men are accounted for without his help. Anaximander thought that fish, as a form of life, preceded land animals, and that man, accordingly, had once been a fish. But as the dry land appeared, some fish adapted themselves to life on land."[13] Again, considering the language used by Anaximenes in positing the primal substance or arche in air, Farrington conjectures, "The idea, to judge by its terminology, was suggested to him by the industrial process of felting woven materials by pressure, and was confirmed by his observation of the process of evaporation and condensation of liquids."[14]

In other words, in contrast to Aristotle, whose inquiry centered on biology, the Ionian philosophers, from Thales to Democritus, investigated the generation of the universe, the emergence of life, the evolution of life forms, and the historical development of human society in a nonteleological way.

Among these figures I would like to give more attention to Empedocles (495–35 BCE) of the Greek colony Acragus in Sicily. He sought to explain the generation of the cosmos according to the combination and separation of four material elements or *rhízōma* (roots); they were water, earth, air, and fire. In his account, first plants, then animals were generated. Here he posits a stage prior to sexual reproduction from which it emerges. His theory is widely regarded as a forerunner of Darwin's ideas of natural selection and the survival of the fittest.

Aristotle touches on Empedocles as follows in the *Physics*: "Wherever then all the parts came about just as they would have been if they had come to be for an end, such things survived, being organized spontaneously in a fitting way; whereas those which grew otherwise perished and continue to perish, as Empedocles says his 'man-faced ox-progeny' did."[15]

Chikatsugu Iwasaki comments on this passage, "When Empedocles uses the term 'adaptive purpose,' it is placed in the context of natural processes, and not based on a simplistic, human-centered teleological view."[16] In other words, the evolution Empedocles discovers is not teleological. Aristotle, though, while incorporating the accomplishments of Ionian natural philosophy, reinterprets them as teleological.

However, even Aristotle's overwhelming influence could not erase the spirit of Ionian thought. This is clear from the accounts of Diodorus of Sicily (first century BCE) quoted by Farrington. In the *Library of History*, Diodorus explains the social and cultural origin of human beings as follows:

Concerning the first generation of the universe this is the account which we have received. But the first men to be born, he says, led an undisciplined and bestial life, setting out one by one to secure their sustenance and taking for their food both the tenderest herbs and the fruits of wild trees. Then, since they were attacked by the wild beasts, they came to each other's aid, being instructed by expediency, and when gathered together in this way by reason of their fear, they gradually came to recognize their mutual characteristics. And though the sounds which they made were at first unintelligible and indistinct, yet gradually they came to give articulation to their speech, and by agreeing with one another upon symbols for each thing which presented itself to them, made known among themselves the significance which was to be attached to each term.

But since groups of this kind arose over every part of the inhabited world, not all men had the same language, inasmuch as every group organized the elements of its speech by mere chance. This is the explanation of the present existence of every conceivable kind of language, and, furthermore, out of these first groups to be formed came all the original nations of the world.

Now the first men, since none of the things useful for life had yet been discovered, led a wretched existence, having no clothing to cover them, knowing not the use of dwelling and fire, and also being totally ignorant of cultivated food. For since they also even neglected the harvesting of the wild food, they laid by no store of its fruits against their needs; consequently large numbers of them perished in the winters because of the cold and the lack of food. Little by little, however, experience taught them both to take to the caves in winter and to store such fruits as could be preserved. And when they had become acquainted with fire and other useful things, the arts also and whatever else is capable of furthering man's social life were gradually discovered. Indeed, speaking generally, in all things it was necessity itself that became man's teacher, supplying in appropriate fashion instruction in every matter to a creature which was well endowed by nature and had, as its assistants for every purpose, hands and speech and sagacity of mind.[17]

As Farrington points out, the Aristotelian notion of man being "by nature a political animal" or "a rational animal" is rejected from first to last in this treatise. Ionian thought became suppressed and overwhelmed by Athenian philosophers like Plato and Aristotle, not so much during their time or under Hellenism, but during the period of the establishment of the Christian church. That is to say, Athenian philosophy survived in Christian theology. The kind of evolutionary theory presented by the Ionians, on the other hand, did not return even with the development of modern physics in the West. The spell of Aristotelean philosophy was not to be fundamentally rejected until Darwin's *On the Origin of Species* (1859).[18]

There were theories of evolution prior to Darwin. Leibniz, for example, perceived an evolution from inorganic materials, to plants, animals, humans, and then God. However, this was not a fundamental break with Aristotle. In other words, evolution is understood from the perspective of God as designer, that is to say, teleologically. What was epoch making about Darwin's theory is that evolution is grasped in the absence of a teleology. We can see this in the fact that Darwin refrained from using the word *evolution*, loaded as it was with teleological connotations, and used instead "descent with modification."

Darwin did not arrive at this kind of thinking through philosophical speculation. He had accumulated a good bit of research about breed improvement (particularly in relation to pigeons), and understood natural selection always in reference to this process. He grappled with the question of how breeding (selection by humans) is different from natural selection (selection by nature). However, this is the same as asking the question of the difference between making and becoming. In other words, Darwin was faced with the same problem as the Ionian natural philosophers and those in their lineage, who sought to understand becoming based on the experience of their productive activities.

Even as Darwin thought of natural selection with reference to breeding, he also drew a distinction between the two. New species are born as a result of random mutation. From among these, as if nature had actually selected them out, certain ones survive. Darwin later explained this borrowing of Spencer's term *survival of the fittest*. However, survival of the fittest is generally understood to imply a fixed directionality or aim to mutation. That is to say, it recuperates the old sense of evolution.

Darwin's epoch-making significance was to place contingency at the basis, and to reject teleology of any kind.[19] In doing so, whether aware or not, Darwin recuperated Ionian thought, which had long been suppressed by Aristotelian thinking.

There is another thinker contemporary with Darwin who gave close attention to Ionian natural philosophy. This would be Marx, who presented to Darwin a copy of *Das Kapital*. Marx's doctoral dissertation was titled "The Difference between the Democritean and Epicurean Philosophies of Nature." Epicurus basically accepted and inherited Democritus's atomism and mechanistic determinism; however, he introduced into atomic motion an unpredictable deviation called a swerve. However, what the young Marx wanted to point out in this thesis was not simply the difference between the two. His real target was Aristotle, who stood in a position antagonistic to both.

Marx situated on the one side Democritus, a sensationalist and mechanistic determinist, and to that degree a skeptic, and on the other the teleological and rationalist Aristotle. In the space between the two, then, he placed Epicurus, a materialist who asserted the random atomic swerve. According to Marx, it is this swerve in atomic motion which, while mechanistic, brings about a variation that appears teleological in effect. In this way the young Marx discovered in Epicurus an attempt to criticize both teleology and mechanistic determinism based on the idea of the atomic swerve. The thought of the Ionian school is revived in this way in Marx's materialism.

In many respects, the thought of the Ionian school remains vital even today. As discussed before, the thinking of the Ionian school, which sees no separation between motion and matter, has been regarded as magical. Indeed, modern physics is built upon their separation. However, as Descartes showed, such a separation is premised on God, or else a godlike perspective. That is to say, on this point modern physics inherits an Aristotelian metaphysics or theology. Quantum mechanics decisively displaces this perspective. In some sense, it recuperates the Ionian position that matter and motion are inseparable. That is to say, the quantum (light, or the electron) is at the same time both particle (matter) and wave (motion).

Chapter 4

Post-Ionian Thought

....

PYTHAGORAS

The Idea of Transmigration

Natural philosophy is not simply an inquiry into nature but an attempt to understand this world from the perspective of physis. It should then be read as a social philosophy as well. Natural philosophy stresses the self-motion of matter and the inseparableness of matter and motion. What would these things signify when read as a social philosophy? It means that the individual existence of human beings is inseparable from their mobility. In other words, without the possibility of movement, there is no individual.

For example, in a society composed of a tribal collective and its extensions, people are subordinate to the community. As a result, no individual exists there. The polis stands on the principle that it is built on consensus or contract among individuals. However, in reality, the Greek city-states were established as federations of various tribes, whose members did not join by choice but were born into them. Individual choice is only possible where individuals are not subject to tribal affiliation and free to move to another place if they so wish. These conditions were present only in colonial cities like Ionia. This was why the principles of the polis originated in Ionia and from there spread to the cities of the Greek mainland.

The citizens of the Ionian polis migrated to get there and could move again whenever they wanted. This is one of the conditions that make possible isonomia (no-rule), where people are equal precisely by virtue of being free. However, as the movement of colonists continues, eventually the requisite frontier will disappear. As the frontier attenuates, gaps in wealth and relations of dominance and submission will emerge interior to the polis. Such tendencies became conspicuous in cities across Ionia in the first half of the sixth century.

Social reforms began appearing at the same time in response. One example occurred on the island of Samos, home to Pythagoras (582–497 BCE), who, with his friend Polycrates, set out to attempt a social reform of the polis. This reform was designed to restore isonomia. However, in order to deal with economic inequality, they had no choice but to adopt majority rule, which is to say, democracy. While this effort achieved success, in the process, Polycrates bit by bit assumed the powers of a tyrant. Pythagoras criticized his friend and left the island of Samos.

After being subjugated by Lydia and Persia, the cities of Ionia became subject to their tyranny as a matter of course, for the installation of tyrants was the standard means of managing city-states under empire. However, it is important to note that tyranny, or conditions close to it, had arisen prior to that in the Ionian cities. It was rather exactly because of this state of affairs that Thales's call for a federation of the poleis fell on deaf ears, and the Ionian cities fell one by one to the neighboring empires. In Athens, the tyranny of Peisistratus arose as a means of breaking the power of the old aristocracy. The tyrant had the support of the people. In Samos, on the other hand, the original state was isonomia, and tyranny arose from within a democracy designed to restore it.

One needs to keep this experience in mind when thinking about Pythagoras. After leaving Samos, Pythagoras led an itinerant life, and various accounts have him visiting Egypt, Persia, central Asia, Gaul, India, and so on. After absorbing knowledge of all kinds, he settled around the age of sixty in the city of Croton in southern Italy and there established an esoteric order. Because of this, Pythagoras's thought was cut off from his experience in Ionia and is seen as originating almost exclusively in these experiences in Asia.

As an example, Pythagoras is said to have introduced the concept of transmigration to the Greek world. According to this doctrine, the soul is originally immortal, that is to say divine in its essence; however, we defile ourselves because of ignorance, and in order to atone for sin the soul is buried in the tomb of the flesh. Our manner of existence on the terrestrial medium that we call life is in fact nothing other than the death of the soul. Unless one regains the original divine nature, one is trapped forever in the cycle of death and rebirth. In order to escape from this cycle the soul must seek knowledge (sophia).

In this sense philo-sophia (or philosophy) is a means of releasing the soul from transmigration. Diogenes Laërtius writes that Pythagoras was the first to use the word *philosophy* (love of knowledge) and the first to identify himself as a philosopher (lover of knowledge). Pythagoras compared life to the festival games, where the spectator is the most desirable position. To be a spectator rather than a competitor means grasping the truth through contemplation or theoria. Plato inherited Pythagoras's thought in a variety of ways. The doctrine of transmigration, for example, is introduced in *Phaedrus*. And in *Phaedo*, the thought of the Pythagoreans on immortality of the soul leads to the theory of ideas. And in *Meno* we find that the theory of recollection (*anamnesis*) relies on Pythagoras's theory of transmigration.

However, notions of transmigration and contemplation are not original to Pythagoras. In Asia, in which he spent his itinerant years, particularly India, these were rather commonplaces. In addition, Orphism, which taught transmigration, had already spread throughout Greece. In Ionia, on the other hand, this kind of thought did not find general acceptance. Pythagoras himself likely would have rejected these ideas. His acceptance of them occurred during his long period of wandering through the various regions of Asia. However, the cause was not the thought of Asia itself, but his own experience in Ionia.

Even in coastal southern Italy, Pythagoras was not the first to advocate the concept of transmigration. The Orphic order was already well established there. Orphism teaches that if one is initiated into its esoteric community, abstains from animal flesh, and accumulates good deeds, a life of happiness and purity awaits in the next world. George Thomson argues that the Pythagorean cult flourished in southern Italy because of the backwardness of the region. "In contrast to the Ionians, whose outlook was predominantly secular and rational, these westerners were noted for the religious cast of their thought and their faith in prophecy and miracles. In this point, they resembled the Hebrews, who also, owing to the circumstances of their history, had kept in touch with their tribal origins."[1] Certainly, one must grant this aspect, which accounts for the popularity of the order of Orpheus, and the ease with which the Pythagorean order sank roots in the region.

However, the question is not of the character of the people of southern Italy, but why Pythagoras, raised in the "remarkably worldly and rational worldview" of Ionia, would take such a turn. The order of Pythagoras bore some resemblance to the Orphic cult, but diverged on a number of points. For example, while the tutelary deity of Orphism was Dionysus, the Pythagorean deity was Apollo, the guardian deity of many Ionian cities. This indicates Pythagoras's strong ties to Ionia. What is even more important is that the Pythagorean movement, though propagated in southern Italy, had its source in Ionia, or, more precisely, in the fall of a remarkably worldly and rational Ionia. To put it another way, it came from Pythagoras's own experience of political frustration.

There is another point that needs to be made in this regard. One should not imagine from the term *contemplation* that Pythagoras has in mind a passive, nonengaged stance toward things. Pythagoras's efforts at social reform in Samos ended in failure. However, after settling in Croton in southern Italy, far from withdrawing in hermetic contemplation, Pythagoras turned again to active social practice.

Certainly, in the Pythagorean order members were obliged to maintain purity, abstain from meat, and practice the fixing of one's attention on the soul in silence. However, unlike Orphism, the Pythagorean movement was political to its core. For example, in Croton, the Pythagoreans became involved in the casting of metal coins and were engaged in the politics of the city, with ties to the rising merchant and manufacturing class as their base. Thomson writes, "The Pythagoreans of Croton not only issued a challenge to accepted notions and traditions but also seized power from the landed aristocracy and used it to promote the development of commodity production."[2] As a result, Croton became the leading polis in southern Italy.

This indicates that Pythagoras did not come to Croton to build an apolitical community of meditation. Quite the contrary, he set about reworking the social reforms here that had failed in Samos. This was the defining factor in the Pythagorean order. Pythagoras set his sights on economic equality for all members, both men and women, in a communistic society. As a result, antagonism inevitably arose between his organization and the state, and finally the organization was suppressed. Its members were scattered to various regions and continued underground as a secret society.

The Dual World

Let us look a little further into Pythagoras's experience in Ionia. What Pythagoras and his friend Polycrates aimed for was a restoration of isonomia to a society riven by class. They adopted democracy (rule by the many) as a means of redistributing wealth. However, what in fact was born from these efforts was tyranny. Pythagoras seems to have understood this to be a result of Polycrates's personal ambition. However, this is not a matter of individual ambition. As a matter of fact, Polycrates himself was not the type to aspire to an authoritarian position. In fact, he is known to later generations through an anecdote told by Herodotus, as a character who undertook a journey to Sardis despite oracular warnings, thereby choosing his own assassination.[3] Polycrates was placed in the position of tyrant rather because of the fervent support of the people of Samos, who demanded a powerful leader who could fulfill their needs and wants.

The nature of the religious order Pythagoras built in southern Italy shows the lessons he drew from his experience in Ionia. First, one cannot entrust things to the people's free will. Doing so will rather result in an authoritarian system that suppresses that very freedom of the people. Second, the leader must be a philosopher, beyond the constraints of the flesh (sensibility). Otherwise, the leader becomes nothing more than a dictator.

The members of the Pythagorean order were thoroughly equal. However, they had no freedom. Here all doctrine originated in Pythagoras himself. He was a guru with absolute authority. In Pythagoras's thought, though, a guru is not a dictator. Moreover, what is commonly understood by freedom is not true freedom. It is a state of being dominated by the body and the sensible. True freedom is realized not in relation to others but by each individual's releasing his or her soul from the prison called the body.

Pythagoras made a clear distinction between knowledge and non-knowledge. In this system, knowledge obtained through the senses is non-knowledge, which true knowledge transcends. For this he is called the first philosopher, or lover of knowledge. However, as with the concept of transmigration, such ideas were commonplace in Asia. Nietzsche had this to say about this kind of theory of a dual world of truth and illusion:

> The very fact that such a distinction is possible—that *this* world should be called the "world of appearance," and the *other world* should be called the "true" world—is symptomatic.

The place of origin of the idea of "another world" is the philosopher.

The philosopher, who invents a rational world, where reason and logical functions are adequate: the "true" world has its origins here.[4]

However, this view does not help us to distinguish the idea of the dual world pervasive in Asia from that of Pythagoras. What is important is that the dual world discerned by Pythagoras is not just another variation of dual-world doctrine. In Pythagoras's case, he arrives at this theory after passing through his experience in an Ionian society where the dual world was rejected. Without taking this into consideration, one cannot capture the inversion and historicity of Pythagoras being hailed as the first philosopher.

The theory of the dual world, or possibly the distinction between those who discern the true world and those who are trapped in the world of the sensible, rests on a division of labor between mental and material. Marx writes as follows:

With [increase in productivity and needs in early society] there develops the division of labour, which was originally nothing but the division of labour in the sexual act, then that division of labour which develops spontaneously or "naturally" by virtue of natural predisposition (e.g., physical strength), needs, accidents, etc., etc. Division of labour only becomes truly such from the moment when a division of material and mental labour appears. [Marx notes in the margin: The first form of ideologists, *priests*, is concurrent.] From this moment onwards consciousness *can* really flatter itself that it is something other than consciousness of existing practice, that it *really* represents something without representing something real; from now on consciousness is in a position to emancipate itself from the world and to proceed to the formation of "pure" theory, theology, philosophy, ethics, etc.[5]

This kind of division of labor is undeveloped in tribal society. However, with the emergence of state society this division appears and ends in the rule of the priestly class. And in fact, in the great civilizations such as Egypt, Babylon, and India, this is what happened. Consequently, the idea of the dual world became a commonplace. However, in Ionia things did not proceed this way. And this was not because Ionia was underdeveloped. The Ionians were thoroughly informed about the presence of this type of highly developed division of labor in the civilizations of Asia but refused it for themselves. While absorbing Asian civilizations in part, they set out to develop their own way.

In the civilizations of Asia, the "first form of ideologists, *priests*," held a monopoly on technical and scientific matters. On the other hand, such a monopoly did not develop in Ionia. In a sense, the power of the priests and bureaucrats was rooted in a monopoly over writing systems that were difficult to acquire, or a monopoly of the knowledge that could be obtained through reading. By contrast, the Ionians adapted Phoenician script into a phonetic alphabet that anyone could easily master. Further, they minted coinage and left trade, pricing, and other matters of economic policy handled by the bureaucracy in the states of Asia to the market. In these circumstances, the bureaucracy and priesthood were not able to sustain any particular authority.

While the cities of Ionia acquired advanced scientific knowledge from Asia, and then developed it further in their own way, this division of material and mental labor never took hold. For instance, the natural philosophers beginning with Thales were not philosophers in Pythagoras's definition. Thales worked as a civil engineer in Egypt and was a mathematician, astronomer, and politician, who developed trigonometry and predicted an eclipse of the sun. The point here is not that Thales was a man of many talents. It is true that his eminence earned him the distinction of sage or a wise man. But he was not a philosopher, as in Ionia there was no such distinction between philosopher and non-philosopher, which is to say that, in Ionia, the dual world was never established.

The cause lay in isonomia. Isonomia tolerates no special status, privilege, or position. When the Ionian natural philosophers eliminated the personified gods of Olympus, they also rejected professional priests and ritualists, which is to say they rejected the implicit division of material and mental labor. This further implies they rejected the dual world, with its distinctions of reason and sensibility, of knowledge and non-knowledge, and of truth and illusion.

The question here is how Pythagoras, who was raised in a landscape of this sort, became the first to advocate the theory of a dual world, or the first philosopher. As mentioned before, it would be off the mark to seek the source of his view in Asia. Pythagoras's idea of the dual world originates in his experience in Ionia. He had aimed at restoring isonomia to a society in which it had collapsed. However, the people he faced were no longer the free and independent citizens of before. They were rather people who would willingly submit to a tyrant. Further, his friend Polycrates, who became that tyrant, also lost the spirit of isonomia, an experience that changed Pythagoras.

Pythagoras had come to reject democracy because of his bitter experience witnessing democracy transform into tyranny. Yet he did not abandon the principle of isonomia itself. He did, however, come to the conclusion that the path lay not in democracy but in the rule of the philosopher. As a result, his pursuit of isonomia ended in the political form in a sense most antithetical to isonomia, and in a philosophy most antithetical to natural philosophy.

Still, we must acknowledge that Pythagoras did pursue isonomia, whether in a self-alienating form or not. The Pythagorean movement was highly political and sought a thorough realization of equality. It was Plato who inherited the legacy of Pythagoras in this connection. Plato's theory of ideas and the concept of the philosopher-king are presented in his dialogues as if they are Socrates's position. However, this is not Socratic, but clearly Pythagorean thinking. What Plato inherits from Pythagoras is not merely mathematics or the concept of transmigration. Pythagorean consciousness rather lies at the core of Plato's political thought.

Plato aspired to be a politician when young, but suffered a decisive setback in the execution of Socrates at the hands of the democratic faction in Athens (399 BCE). For Plato, who by reason of family status was aligned with the nobility, this incident effectively blocked his path to public life. From this point, all that was left was the path of the philosopher. Plato subsequently, like Pythagoras, exiled himself from Athens and commenced an itinerant period, finally studying in Tarentum in southern Italy with the Pythagorean school. The academy Plato would establish in Athens was of course based on this, but neither is that the extent of the legacy. Plato found in the politics of the Pythagoreans the skepticism he had long held toward democracy, as well as the key to its transcendence.

Mathematics and Music

That Pythagoras originated in an Ionian political context is generally disregarded. This misses his origin in an Ionian intellectual context as well. Cornford, for example, argues that the origin of philosophy needs to be located in the mystic cults and magical traditions and finds the source of Pythagoras's thinking in the shamanism of northern Greece.[6] However, this misses the point in the same way as the reduction of Pythagoras's thought to notions of transmigration or body/spirit dualism circulating in Asia, namely, that Pythagoras's roots were in the Ionian intellectual traditions. Pythagoras did indeed affirm the dual world. However, he sought the basis of this less in transmigration than in mathematics. This indicates a line of thought that is prototypically Ionian in nature. However, Pythagoras sought to reject this tradition from the inside.

Mathematics was originally developed as a practical science in Asia. However, as with writing and reading, it was a form of knowledge monopolized by the priestly class. For example, mathematics in Egypt was developed from the necessity to survey real property holdings after the seasonal floods of the Nile. From this was born geodesy as geometry, but these studies were conducted by the priests and were not made public. Another source of mathematics was the development of Babylonian astronomy. This too developed from the necessities of large-scale irrigated agriculture, but its research was advanced by the priesthood in a form indistinguishable from astrology. In Ionia, though, knowledge was not a monopoly of the priesthood. While advances in astronomy from Babylonia were incorporated, the astrology that tied it to magic and the priesthood did not find acceptance. The Ionians had banished the gods from the scene.

In that sense, the mathematics developed by Thales and others was practical and not at all mystical. The reason for the proliferating interest in mathematics in Ionia lay above all in the development of the money economy. Here, the value of all things is quantified in terms of currency. Naturally, number becomes fundamental. The fact that the Pythagoreans in Croton were involved in casting metal currency is a result of Pythagoras's Ionian background. And Pythagoras was first exposed to mathematics in this climate. That is to say, mathematics for him was originally a practical pursuit.

However, after Pythagoras departed Ionia, mathematics began to lose this practicality and acquire a mystical character. He put mathematics to use rather in relation to music and astronomy. This was not because of an interest in their utility, though both fields found practical applications. For the Pythagoreans, music in particular was regarded as a means of purifying and releasing the soul from the cycle of reincarnation. For example, the mathematical achievement for which Pythagoras is best known is the elucidation of the mysteries of interval and intonation. Through an empirical process of varying the string length of the monochord, he discovered the principal intervals in the musical scale to be exact proportional relations, that is to say, octave = 2:1, fifth = 3:2, fourth = 4:3, and so on.

Needless to say, chords were in practical use before Pythagoras. What he made clear was that the secret of the magical power of music lay in the proportional relations of number.[7] In other words, his thinking was not magical, but highly rational and, in that sense, still Ionian. On the other hand, it was also anti-utilitarian. For example, he is most famous for the Pythagorean theorem; however, this was not his discovery. We know from material preserved in clay tablets that the basic relations were already well known in Babylonia. Indeed, a form of algebra had already been developed by the Babylonians for practical reasons, and there was systematic speculation on the quadratic equations. By contrast, as we see with the Pythagorean theorem, his obsession with integers closed off the possibilities of algebra. The inheritors of Pythagorean mathematics such as Plato and Euclid were able to advance mathematics as a matter of logical proof, but made no contribution to the development of applied mathematics.

Pythagoras applied himself to astronomy as well. In Babylonia astronomy advanced as a part of the field of astrology, that is to say, as a means of reading earthly phenomena in terms of the movement of stars. This had a mystical bent, but was at the same time rooted in an instrumental goal. Pythagoras did not share this kind of motivation. The sole interest of Pythagoras was to discover the mathematical structure hidden in celestial motions.

Astronomy is one of the fields of inquiry that most privileges mathematics. The heavenly bodies cannot be discovered as objects, but only as relations or laws of transformation. For example, prior to the advent of astronomy as a systematic study, people knew of the constellations and the legends on which they were based. To know a constellation is to grasp an unchanging structure out of the ceaselessly changing position of the stars scattered in the night sky. Of course, people discerned the constellations from very early on without being aware of their structure, just as they utilized chords and harmonies without being aware that they were based on exact proportional relations. Pythagoras, however, elucidated the secret of the harmonies. In the same way, he thought he could make clear the secret of the celestial motions. For him, astronomy was a matter of listening to the music of the spheres. When an instrument is tuned a certain number of octaves higher, it becomes inaudible to human ears. Conversely, though inaudible to humans, through a mathematical realization we can know the music of the spheres. This is a music that transcends the senses.

It was from this point that Pythagoras began advocating the idea of a dual world (the sensible world, and a world beyond the senses). That is to say, the dual-world theory came out of mathematics. The point of mathematics is to grasp the relation of one object to another. Thinking this way, we encounter a problem. Objects exist, and the relation of object to object also exists. But does the latter exist in the same sense that the objects themselves exist?

For example, in the case of harmony, if individual sounds do not exist, then their proportions do not exist either. Conversely, if there is no proportion (i.e., relation) between them, sounds cannot become music. However individual sounds might vary, such relational structures remain the same. The following question then arises. Does the relationship between sounds exist in the same way as sounds themselves exist? Just so, Pythagoras replies. Not only that, true existence lies in the latter. In this way, Pythagoras arrived at the idea of a dual world from a mathematical consciousness. This indicates that his dual world is different from notions of the dual world already in circulation, based on transmigration, immortality of the soul, and so on.

Pythagoras located the arche (the principle of things) in number. As outlined before, at the same time this conforms with the basic attitude of Ionian natural philosophy, it is a fundamental rejection of it. This is because what Pythagoras discerned as fundamental was not physis. Pythagoras viewed number as reality. Numbers are about relationships, and their mode of existence is not the same as that of individual material things. To see relations as more real notwithstanding, and then locate in them the arche, is to identify abstraction as reality. In Pythagoras, Ionian natural philosophy was converted de facto to a form of idealism.

Hegel understood Pythagoras's identification of number as reality as the first step to the theory of ideas. Hegel sees number as standing midway between sensuous things and thought. Number is only a beginning of thought, but a beginning in the worst possible way. In other words, Pythagoras had not yet reached the level of pure thought. According to

Hegel, the level of thought is first attained with the Ideas of Plato. However, the real state of affairs is exactly the reverse. Plato's theory of Ideas only came into being by taking Pythagoras's identification of number as reality as a premise.

For instance, Plato offers as an example of the Idea the notion of a horse. In Plato's thinking, individual horses exist in their variety, but each partakes imperfectly of the Idea of a horse that exists in another dimension. However, to approach Ideas from this kind of example is not fitting. In fact, the identification of Idea and concept here is easy to refute, as we see when Socrates's pupil Antisthenes says, "Plato, I see particular horses, but not horseness." Aristotle criticized Plato's idealism in the same way, arguing that individual things alone are real, and the concept is discovered only through the observation of individual things. However, Plato could never have arrived at the notion of Ideas, that is to say a reality different from sensible reality, from such a standpoint. He grasped the Ideas not through the existence of individual things but through the relationships among them as reality, that is to say through mathematical reasoning.

It is clear that Plato sought the basis of idealism in mathematics, and it is famously reported that a sign hung at the Academy gates that read, "Let no man ignorant of geometry enter here." Insofar as mathematics is concerned, it is not easy to reject the ideas. And even if one does so, one cannot reject the fact that relation exists independently from individual things. Greek contributions to modern science are not limited to the atomic theory of Democritus and Epicurus, but include as well the kind of thinking that would say, "the book of nature is written in the language of mathematics," a conception attributed to Galileo but in fact rooted in Pythagoras. Copernicus's heliocentric theory is rooted as well in Pythagoras.[8]

As to why one should be able to apprehend the foundation of the world through mathematics, this remains a mystery. All we can do is to simply acknowledge it. As an example, in the most current ideas in particle physics, the fundamental particles exist only mathematically. In other words, they exist only as a set of relations. In this case, it is impossible to determine if they are ultimately matter or relation. Consequently, one cannot easily dismiss Pythagoras's thought that the basis of all things is number. Still, one can and must reject the implication from there that we live in a world of duality, composed of the sensible and the ideal.

Against the Masses

A standard interpretation is that Heraclitus was an aristocratic thinker who scorned the general populace. Karl Popper's critique of Heraclitus is representative. According to Popper, as a member of the aristocratic class, Plato was an ideologue who upheld the traditions of the tribal aristocracies, and Heraclitus anticipated him in this. "Heraclitus, the first philosopher to deal not only with 'nature' but even more with ethico-political problems, lived in an age of social revolution. It was in his time that the Greek tribal aristocracies were beginning to yield to the new force of democracy."[9]

Popper is wrong here on two counts. First, Heraclitus was certainly not "the first philosopher to deal "not only with 'nature' but even more with ethico-political problems." As I argued before, the natural philosophers were already engaged in this sort of task. Second, Heraclitus did not live in an age when "the Greek tribal aristocracies were beginning to yield to the new force of democracy." Quite the contrary. Popper's view is simply the usual Athenocentric understanding of the history of democracy.

The slightest attention to Ionian history makes it clear that Heraclitus did not live in such an age. The Ionian city-states had been incorporated into the Lydian empire in 561 BCE and then further subjugated by the Persians in 548. The politics of isonomia that had characterized the Ionian states were dismantled, replaced by tyrants affiliated with the Persian Empire. These are the social conditions in which Heraclitus (540–ca. 480 BCE) was born and raised. Far from an age when "the Greek tribal aristocracies were beginning to yield to the new force of democracy," he was raised in an age when isonomia was only a distant memory.

Why does this sort of misreading represented by Popper arise? First, Heraclitus is believed to have been the eldest son of the Ephesian nobility or high aristocracy. However, Ephesus was a city formed by immigrants, and there was no trace of the tribal system that makes possible the rule by aristocracy or royalty. An aristocracy in this case must have been something like a lineage of the leaders who worked to protect the freedom of citizens. Heraclitus calls these leaders the "superior men." "One man is worth ten thousand to me, if he is superior."[10] The duty of the superior man was not to rule over others but to protect the autonomy of the polis. However, that was a task Heraclitus himself did not fulfill—or, more accurately, was not able to fulfill. It is said that Heraclitus ceded this position to his younger brother, but such leadership was impossible in any case under subjection to the Lydians and the Persians.

The image of Heraclitus as a haughty aristocrat lies, second, in the volley of scorn and abuse he heaped on the Ephesian citizenry. "The adult citizens of Ephesus should hang themselves, every one, and leave the city to children" (143, B121).[11] "May your wealth not cease, men of Ephesus, that your wickedness may be exposed" (145, B125a). Popper discovers there a hostility toward democracy and a contempt for the people, a legacy that is then inherited by Plato. However, as clear as it might be that Plato, a member of the aristocratic class in Athens, nursed a hostility toward democracy, it misses the mark to seek an antecedent in Heraclitus.

Heraclitus's Ephesus was different from other Ionian city-states, many of which had fought against the rule of their Persia-affiliated tyrants and established democratic government in their place. This is the Ionian Revolt (499–93 BCE). These rebellions hoped to enlist the power of Athens in their cause; however, this was not sufficiently forthcoming, and the revolt ended in devastating defeat. Miletus, Ionia's principal city and home to Thales and others, was reduced to ashes and appears never to have recovered. Only Ephesus survived this period. It distanced itself from the rebellion and judiciously maneuvered for survival. It would not be until the defeat of the Persians by the Greek federation in the Greco-Persian War that the citizens of Ephesus would find themselves again federated with the Greek people. Hideya Yamakawa writes, "Compared to the tragedy that befell Miletus, one could only call the fate of Ephesus fortunate. Still, this does not change the fact that Heraclitus, a man filled with pride and fierce character, passed his whole life in a turbulent age of 'lost freedom' and humiliating 'servitude' to the Persians."[12]

Rather than fighting against Persia together with other poleis, the Ephesian people accepted subjugation for the sake of survival. Heraclitus despised such a people and hurled abuse at them. Is this reaction really best understood as antidemocratic and aristocratic, though? In Ephesus's case, government by tyrants and subjugation to the Persians was in accordance with the will of the people. If democracy consists in going along with the will of such a people, Heraclitus was indeed antidemocratic. Nevertheless, his abhorrence for the people or, shall we say, antidemocracy, was not a stance against isonomia or Ionian thought. Isonomia, or no-rule, is not just a rejection of ruler-ruled relations internal to the state, but by definition includes a rejection of foreign rule. This means that the essential condition of isonomia is first of all independence. If one avoids the need to fight for that, there can be no isonomia. For Heraclitus, "The people of a city should fight for their laws as they would for their city walls" (138, B44).

The Ephesians sat out the Ionian Revolt and passed their days in relative tranquility in a state of dependence. Heraclitus despised such a peace, because it meant resigning oneself to subordination. The surviving fragments of Heraclitus are filled with words of praise for war and battle. "War is father of all and king of all; and some he aligns with the gods, some he places in the ranks of men; some he made slaves, some free" (59, B53). One needs to keep in mind that these words were addressed to an Ephesus which, without a fight, had exchanged its independence for a state of dependency and security.

The Ephesians witnessed the revolt and destruction of the other Ionian peoples as they survived in peace. Heraclitus avers that "Gods and men honor those slain in war" (118, B24). However, there was no opportunity for such honor among the Ephesians. "There is a single common world for those who are awake, but each sleeper retires into a private world" (9, B89). The Ephesians turned their back on the common world of the polis and retired into sleep. "The best choose one thing in place of all, immortal fame above what must perish; the many gorge themselves like cattle" (125, B29).

It is quite clear Heraclitus inherits the legacy of Ionian philosophy. As Thales found the arche in water, and Anaximenes in air, so Heraclitus discovered it in fire. In Heraclitus's thought, all the elements—earth, water, air—are transformations of fire. Heraclitus is regarded by some to have advanced a step beyond natural philosophy with this. However, this is not particularly different from Anaximenes identifying the arche as air. If there were a difference, it would be that Heraclitus regarded fire not only as the primary element but as a metaphor for battles as well. Nevertheless, this kind of treatment of arche was not unique to Heraclitus but typical of the Ionian school.

Heraclitus criticized the cult of Bacchus, with its ecstatic devotees, magicians, and esoteric practice: "For whom does Heraclitus prophesy? Night-wanderers, magi, Bacchants, Lenaeans, initiates; these he threatens with things after death; for these he prophesies fire. For the mysteries traditionally practiced by men are celebrated in an unholy manner" (158, B14). This is obviously in line with Ionian iconoclasm, and at the same time a rejection of the Pythagoreans. Here it becomes clear that Heraclitus's inheritance of Ionian thought is not simply a matter of the understanding of nature. Natural philosophy was at the same time social philosophy.

As quoted earlier, Anaximander introduced the principle of justice (or *dikē*) as the law governing the natural world. "From what things existing objects come to be, into them too does their destruction take place, according to what must be: for they give recompense and pay restitution to each other for their injustice according to the ordering of time."[13] Anaximander here is said to imply that all things come into being out of strife, violating the equilibrium of dikē, thus ending in retributive extinction. If we read this as a statement of social philosophy, Anaximander appears to understand strife to be injustice.

By contrast, for Heraclitus, it is precisely in strife that justice is found. "We must recognize that war is common, strife is justice, and all things happen according to strife and necessity" (58, B80). That is to say, to avoid conflict and struggle is to bring about extinction. One cannot explain the divergence of opinion between the two on this point simply as a matter of one's understanding of nature. The difference between Anaximander and Heraclitus reflects the difference between Ionia at one time and the Ionia that was to follow. Anaximander developed his thought in a Miletus where isonomia was in the process of collapsing, Heraclitus in an Ephesus that had avoided conflict to live in subjection to Persia.

Against Pythagoras

In understanding Heraclitus, the most important distinction to be drawn is with Pythagoras. In fact, Heraclitus was quite conscious of Pythagoras. In his fragments we find negative references to Pythagoras in two places. "Pythagoras, son of Mnesarchus, practiced inquiry more than all men, and making a framework to sort others' writings, he invented these as his own type of wisdom: information-gathering, fraud!" (22, B129). What in Pythagoras might Heraclitus see fit to label fraud?

This charge too needs to be understood in the context of its relation to Ionian politics and natural philosophy. As outlined before, Pythagoras departed Ionia after a series of political setbacks, commencing an itinerant period in which he did his information gathering, and then founded an academy in Croton in southern Italy. And while inheriting Ionian natural philosophy in some sense, the discernment of number as the principle of all things led him to discard Ionian materialism and turn to a world of ideals. Pythagoras made a distinction between phenomena that can be grasped by the senses, and mathematical knowledge that can only be arrived at through reason (*logos*). The Platonic dual world (consisting of the sensible world of illusion and the eternal world of reason) has its origins here.

Heraclitus rejected this. Above all, he sought to maintain the natural philosophical position emphasizing matter and its inherent motion. What he terms "fire" is matter at the same time that it is motion. It goes without saying that this way of thinking has its roots in Ionian philosophy. The influence of Xenophanes (ca. 570–480 BCE) is particularly evident here. Xenophanes is known for his scorn of anthropomorphism, arguing that if cows or horses could speak, they would represent their gods in the form of cows or horses. What is important here is that he discerned the basis of his criticism of anthropomorphism in "One God." "One God, greatest among gods and men, not at all like to mortals in body nor in thought."[14]

This One God, though, was not something outside this world. For Xenophanes, it was precisely nature, or this world, that was God. According to Aristotle, "Xenophanes, the first of these partisans of the One, gave no clear statement . . . but with reference to the whole material universe he says the One is God."[15] This, however, is a rejection of gods or the true world outside nature, which is tantamount to a rejection of the dual world.

Heraclitus follows this line of thinking. It is certainly the case that he placed great emphasis on change, multiplicity, and strife. This is the Heraclitus whose name has become synonymous with the idea that all things flow. However, this kind of thinking is not itself unique in this context. What is important is rather the understanding that emerges from it. Pythagoras set in opposition to this ceaselessly changing world of sensible realities an eternal and incorruptible world. At first glance, Heraclitus seems to be saying the same thing. He too claims that all things are one, and opposing things are also one. "Wisdom is one thing: to know the will that steers all things through all" (40, B41). "Having hearkened not to me but to the Word [logos], you should agree that wisdom is knowing that all things are one" (41, B50). Nevertheless, this does not in any way indicate that there is, behind this transient world of sense impressions, a world of essential unity. Quite the opposite, the purport is that any kind of world one can conceive beyond this one world is only an illusion.

What Heraclitus terms the One is nothing other than this world, as cosmos. "This world-order, the same of all, no god nor man did create, but it ever was and is and will be: ever living fire, kindling in measures and being quenched in measures" (47, B30). Heraclitus's thinking here clearly derives from Xenophanes's notion of the World as the One. The One here is God, which however is not to be anthropomorphized. Heraclitus states, "One being, the only wise one, would and would not be called by the name of Zeus (life)" (147, B32).

What is unique to Heraclitus lies in the notion that "the One is generated from the totality of things; the totality of things is generated from the One." What he expresses here by "the One" is different from the idea of an essential identity hidden on the horizon of external appearance. For Heraclitus, the One does not exist beyond materiality and motion, but comes to be realized through motion. As mentioned before, the motion of matter for Heraclitus meant the strife of opposing things. One may add to this that the motion of matter takes the form of the exchange of opposing things. "All things are an exchange for fire and fire for all things, as goods for gold and gold for goods" (55, B90).

According to Heraclitus, fire occupies a position in relation to all things just as money (gold) does. However, his point is not that fire is special and different in kind from all things. Fire too is a member of the set. The transcendence of fire notwithstanding is through social exchange with the totality of things. This reasoning is identical to Marx's analysis of money in *Capital*. That is to say, gold becomes a currency not through its intrinsic properties, but through a social exchange with all things that places gold in the position of general equivalent.[16]

Pythagoras discovered the arche or original element of all things in number. At the same time he inherits the question of arche from Ionian natural philosophy, this is a fundamental rejection of the tradition. This is because he erased the idea of self-moving matter at the center of natural philosophy. By contrast, as we see above, Heraclitus's thought is a recovery of Ionian natural philosophy. However, the difference between Pythagoras and Heraclitus does not lie simply in the response to natural philosophy. It lies more fundamentally in the response to the collapse of Ionian society.

When the polis of Samos bent its knee to the tyrannical system, Pythagoras set out for a new land to build an ideal society unswayed by the sensible. The Pythagorean order was the result. This was to recuperate the lost isonomia in an alienated ideal form. This would later return in Plato's idea of the philosopher-king.

By contrast, Heraclitus never gave up on his polis. He continued to demand isonomia despite all evidence to the contrary. Naturally, he was a nuisance to the contemporary Ephesians and always stood alone. What is worth noting here is rather that, in an age when numerous thinkers, not only Pythagoras, left their poleis and wandered from place to place, Heraclitus never left Ephesus his entire life despite his detestation of it. He was certainly not a person whose vision was confined to the scope of the polis. He was an uncompromising individualist and cosmopolitan. What he names by *logos* is a universal thing held in common, that transcends the laws of the polis. "Speaking with sense we must fortify ourselves in the common sense of all, as a city is fortified by its law, and even more forcefully. For all human laws are nurtured by the one divine law. For it prevails as far as it will and suffices for all and is superabundant" (139, B114). "That is why one must follow the common. Although this Word [logos] is common, the many live as if they had a private understanding" (9, B2).

Yet Heraclitus remained in his polis. This is because it was precisely in the polis that what he called logos must be realized. Isonomia is realized in the small polis. And a federation of such poleis constitutes a cosmopolis. However, if such poleis do not exist, a cosmopolis can lead only to something like a world empire. In fact, the type of thinkers who fled their polis developed an individualist philosophy suited to the empire of the Hellenistic period. By contrast, Heraclitus remained in the Ephesus he so relentlessly criticized.

This kind of behavior by Heraclitus resembles that of Socrates, who declined to flee Athens and remained even after receiving the death sentence. Plato in the *Republic* states that the duty of a citizen lies in fidelity to the nomos of the polis and, further, that this nomos is realized through the direction of one superior individual. He attributes this kind of thinking to Heraclitus. However, Heraclitus was not the leader of a collective, nor did he aim to be. The same holds true of Socrates, whom Plato admires. We can gather from this that Plato's thought has its basis neither in Heraclitus nor in Socrates, but in Pythagoras. And like Pythagoras,

Plato sought to realize his own ideal state not in Athens, but externally, in Syracuse.

....

Heraclitus and Parmenides

Parmenides is typically regarded as having played the most important role in the shift from Ionian natural philosophy to Athenian philosophy. However, this view is chiefly that of the Athenian philosophers. It seems rather, to me, that what brought about a decisive shift in Ionian philosophy was Pythagoras, and that Heraclitus and Parmenides were figures that resisted this change. It is clear at a glance that the combative political stance and ties to natural philosophy place Heraclitus close to the Ionian school, but the case of Parmenides is not so clear. The method of indirect proof he developed seems like a new element not found in the Ionian thinkers. Plato utilized this as a weapon to unseat Ionian natural philosophy. In fact, however, indirect proof has its origins in Ionia as well.

Parmenides had deep ties to Ionia. He was a citizen of Elea, a Greek colony settled by Ionian immigrants. He is said to have been influenced by the Pythagorean school and taken residence with its order for a time. This story has the effect of separating Parmenides from the tradition of the Ionian school. On the other hand, Aristotle writes in the *Metaphysics*, "It is said that Parmenides was a pupil of Xenophanes." Pythagoras, despite his Ionian origin, rejected Ionian philosophy. The Ionian Xenophanes, on the other hand, placed himself completely within its lineage. Consequently, to affirm one of these accounts seems to entail rejecting the other. However, there is no need to make a choice. It becomes coherent if we understand that Parmenides received early training with the Pythagorean school and then became a pupil of Xenophanes, a critic of the Pythagoreans who immigrated from Ionia. This is to see the lifelong task of Parmenides as lying in overcoming Pythagorean thought, to which he had at one time devoted himself, from a position internal to it. This indicated as well a recuperation of Ionian thinking.

We need to examine another deep-seated prejudice in this respect. Parmenides said, "What-is is, for being is, and nothing is not."[17] That is to say, one cannot simultaneously exist and not exist. Heraclitus, on the other hand, says, "All things are in flux." "Into the same rivers we step and do not step, we are and are not" (65, B49a). There seems to be an opposition or criticism here to Parmenides's formulation. This was Hegel's understanding. Based on this view, Hegel treated Heraclitus as a thinker subsequent to Parmenides:

> With the Eleatics [for Hegel principally Xenophanes, Parmenides, and Zeno], we have the abstract understanding that Being is alone the truth; however, this universal principle is better characterized as Becoming, the truth of Being. Being is merely the first, direct notion to be thought. . . . Heraclitus states that all is Becoming; this is the universal principle. To pass from Being to Becoming demonstrates a great boldness of thought. Even if, as the unity of opposite determinations it is still abstract, it represents the first step toward the concrete. Because in this opposition of being and nonbeing both must be unrestful and contain within themselves the vivid principle of life. The concept of movement—which Aristotle had demonstrated to be lacking in earlier philosophies—is supplied, and this last is even made to be the principle.[18]

Heraclitus is estimated to have lived from circa 540–480 BCE, Parmenides from about 515–450 BCE, so it is nearly impossible that Heraclitus's work was meant as a rebuttal to Parmenides. On this point, Hegel's *History of Philosophy* is wrong. Could we then posit the reverse, that Parmenides was expressing a difference with Heraclitus? This seems unlikely as well. To the contrary, on a number of points they actually agree. Both, rather, can be understood as struggling against the Pythagorean thought that precedes them.

Hegel, relying on Aristotle, finds Heraclitus to be supplying an idea of motion that was lacking in prior philosophy. This too, though, is mistaken. Ionian natural philosophy discovered the arche in self-moving matter. Here, matter and motion are inseparable. It is Pythagoras, rather, who separated them. For Pythagoras, what exists at the basis of matter is the kind of relation grasped in mathematics. From this was born the idea of a knowledge different from sensible knowledge, or a real world different from the sensible world. This is further to see the world as static. Consequently, motion is only illusion. What appears to us as motion is simply the multiplication of number from the one to the many. Heraclitus objected to this kind of thinking.

Heraclitus identified fire in its material aspect as the source of all things, and emphasized its ceaseless motion or becoming. Here he recuperates the Ionian natural philosophy inherited through Xenophanes. But what of Parmenides in this connection? His doctrine of the One gave rise to the general view that he denied mobility. However, as I will develop in detail, what he actually denied was rather the Pythagorean view of the dual world. Parmenides thought that if we take the Pythagorean view, motion cannot exist. This was a rejection not of mobility, but of the static view of the world. If Heraclitus, in response to the Pythagoreans, can be said to have directly affirmed self-moving matter, Parmenides affirmed it through the method of indirect proof.

Another point that needs to be made in relation to Heraclitus and Parmenides is that their critiques of Pythagoras were not merely theoretical. Hegel writes as follows: "Heraclitus flourished about the 69th Olympiad (500 B.C.), and was of Ephesus and in part contemporaneous with Parmenides: he began the separation and withdrawal of philosophers from public affairs and the interests of the country, and devoted himself in his isolation entirely to Philosophy."[19] It is true that Heraclitus never held public office, but one has to say that his interests and activities were consistently public in nature. As for Parmenides's public service, all we have is the fragment by Diogenes Laërtius, "He is also said to have given laws to his fellow citizens, as Speusippus records." However, we are able to infer Parmenides's political stance from the behavior of his loyal disciple, adopted son, and lover Zeno.

Zeno is known as the author of the paradoxes, and forerunner to the Sophists, but Diogenes Laërtius reports a number of rather surprising stories. For example, when Zeno was apprehended for plotting the overthrow of the tyrant Nearkos, he is said to have reported that he had a secret meant only for the tyrant's ears. When he drew near, he bit into the tyrant's ear and would not let go until he was stabbed. Other accounts have that he bit the nose off. A second version goes as follows: "He was asked by the tyrant if there was anyone else [involved in the plot]. And he replied, 'Yes, you, the destruction of the city.' And that he also said to the bystanders, 'I marvel at your cowardice, if you submit to be slaves to the tyrant out of fear of such pains as I am now enduring.' And at last he bit off his tongue and spit it at him; and the citizens immediately rushed forward, and slew the tyrant with stones."[20]

"I marvel at your cowardice." As with the case of Heraclitus, it misses the mark to call this saying an elitism that scorns the masses. Quite the opposite—Zeno's words come from the spirit of isonomia. Further, Zeno's agitation spurred the citizens to movement and realized the overthrow of the tyrant. Parmenides, whom this person looked up to as a master, was no doubt as combative a personality as Heraclitus. Though the works by Parmenides we are left may appear abstract and enigmatic, they are far from evidence of "the separation and withdrawal of philosophers from public affairs and the interests of the country." That is to say, he was not at all a contemplative figure in the Pythagorean way. His statement "and nothing is not" is linked to his rejection of the contemplation of "nothing." Still, his critique of Pythagoras was not confined merely to the theoretical level.

Critique of Pythagoras

Aristotle summarizes the thought of Parmenides as follows.

> Parmenides seems in places to speak with [more] insight. For, claiming that, besides the existent, nothing non-existent exists, he thinks that of necessity what exists is one, viz. the existent and nothing else. . . . But being forced to follow the observed facts, and supposing the existence of that which is one in definition, but more than one according to our sensations, he now posits two causes and two principles, calling them hot and cold, i.e. fire and earth; and of these he ranges the hot with the existent, and the cold with the non-existent.[21]

This statement indicates rather Parmenides's debt to Ionian philosophy. Aristotle states that for Parmenides, "what exists [what Is] is one [*einai, to on*]"; however, "being forced to follow the observed facts," he accepted the multiplicity of the sensible world. This explanation does not stand to reason. Parmenides never rejected the world of sense to begin with. When he asserts that "what exists is one," it is not against the Ionian school. It is rather directed to Pythagoras, who rejected the world of the senses and introduced the idea of the void.

The Ionian thinkers rejected Hesiod's myth that the world was generated out of Chaos (the void). They did not agree on what the original matter might be, but commonly held that nothing is generated from the void, nor is anything extinguished. Pythagoras on the other hand held that the origin of all things was not matter of any kind, but number. One, then, is born from the void (for Pythagoras *kenon*, the empty), and reabsorbed into the void, whence is generated the Many. One might express this in contemporary mathematical terms as number being generated from the null set. However, in the context of ancient Greece, this is a reintroduction of the mythological thinking that the world is born out of Chaos. By contrast, Parmenides rejects the view that the world is generated out of the void or nothing. The void is nothing (what-is-not). And nothing is not. What-is, on the other hand, is One. This means, as it were, the permanence of matter. Rejecting the idea of generation from the void or nothingness is a critique of pre-Ionian thought (Hesiod), as well as post-Ionian thought (Pythagoras), and in that sense a recuperation of Ionian thought.

To reiterate, Parmenides's claims are not a rejection of motion or becoming. On the contrary, he attempted to recover the natural philosophical vision of matter that moves by itself. As mentioned before, Pythagoras rejected motion. In his vision, at the foundation of all things lies relation, and this relation is static. This is a contrast to the thought of the Ionian school, and marks rather a return to pre-Ionian thought represented by Hesiod.

In mythology, all things are seen in retrospect. In other words, events that have already happened are interpreted to be the result of the will or the design of the gods. If this is the case, what Ionian natural philosophy rejected was not the gods in themselves, but the post-factum or teleological perspective of events. They grasped the motion of matter in a nonteleological way, hence giving rise to a form of evolution. In Pythagoras, however, motion is interpreted post-factum. And it is precisely this retrospectively discovered world that for him is the real world. This view then extends its reach to produce Plato's theory of Ideas and the demiurges (designers of the universe), as well Aristotle's ideas of final and formal causes.

What Parmenides rejected was the retrospective viewpoint introduced by Pythagoras. Retrospectively, one can understand motion to be a combination of number and point. To put it another way, a continuous line can be resolved into number and point, and likewise number and point combine to form something continuous. What Parmenides maintained is that motion is indivisible, that is to say, One. He sought to show this by indirect proof, and his pupil Zeno employed the same method. According to Plato's *Parmenides*, when the Pythagoreans ridiculed Parmenides's idea of the One Being, Zeno rose to Parmenides's defense, countering that absurdity follows from supposing the existence of the Many. Zeno's paradoxes are taken to demonstrate the impossibility of multiplicity or motion. In fact it is the opposite; he demonstrates that multiplicity and motion are impossible if one holds the view of the Pythagoreans. In other words, Zeno's paradoxes are aimed to refute the Pythagorean school at the premise.

For example, the paradox of Achilles and the tortoise has the following purpose. If one hypothesizes that a linear continuum is infinitely divisible, it follows that Achilles would never be able to overtake the tortoise, because each time Achilles arrives at where the tortoise was a moment before, the tortoise has advanced further. In reality, however, Achilles will overtake the tortoise. Thus, a continuum cannot be infinitely divided. In other words, the world is, as Parmenides said, "the One Being." Again, in the famous paradox of the flying arrow at rest, the argument goes like this: if we take an arrow in motion, and divide its motion into instants, for each of those moments, the arrow is at rest. If the period of the arrow's motion is composed entirely of such moments, the arrow is at rest throughout its flight. In reality, though, arrows do fly. Consequently, it is mistaken to think of the arrow at rest, that is to say, matter severed from motion.

Zeno's paradoxes are not meant to demonstrate the impossibility of motion. Rather, they are a demand for a line of thought that would enable motion. In *Time and Free Will*, Bergson asserts that, while space is divisible, time is indivisible duration. However, according to him, the view that time can be treated in the same way as space had dominated philosophy till then. He lays the responsibility for this confusion to, of all things, the Eleatic thinkers. It was precisely the Eleatics, though, who were the first to critique the view of time and motion as divisible.

In my way of thinking, Bergson's spatialization of time indicates the observation of motion after its completion. As an example, this moment is usually understood to occupy a position between the past and the future. However, that is to see this moment retrospectively. As soon as we say "this moment," it is already gone. In the true now, it is not just that past and present do not exist; even now does not exist. It is what Parmenides called the One Being. This is to see motion, becoming, and transformation, in the midst of its arising.

Hegel regarded Zeno as the father of the dialectic. However, Zeno's dialectic comes to life at the moment of scrutinizing a proposition temporarily accepted to be true. Then, the purpose of his method was to refute the perspective that views motion after the fact. By contrast, the Hegelian dialectic is designed to reconstitute motion from a retrospective position. This kind of thinking descends from Pythagoras and Plato, and is rather foreign to Heraclitus and Parmenides.

Indirect Proof

Parmenides proved the proposition "nothing is not" by demonstrating that holding its antithesis, "nothing is," leads one to paradox. Zeno, then, proved the existence of the indivisible One by showing that one falls into absurdity if one tries to divide it into parts. This type of indirect proof is thought to have been invented by the Eleatics and thereby to indicate a break with Ionian thought. However, as outlined before, Parmenides did not try to reject natural philosophy, but rather to indirectly affirm it. This method of indirect proof itself, as well, was not invented by Parmenides, but was already present in Ionian natural philosophy.

Natural philosophy is not just a matter of empirical observation. Any kind of practical knowledge originates in a hypothesis, which is then critically examined (*elenchos*) and revised accordingly. What originated and developed in Ionia was this habit of leading with a hypothesis. According to Yamakawa, "Parmenides was not the first to display the prototypical deductive character of Greek science; this was present in germ in Ionian science from the start."[22] For example, when Anaximander discerns as the arche the apeiron (the boundless), he makes his case by showing that if one limits the arche by defining it as water or fire, it becomes logically inconsistent. This is the method of indirect proof.

According to Aristotle, Xenophanes too demonstrated God or the One by indirect proof: "For instance, it was a saying of Xenophanes that to assert that the gods had birth is as impious as to say that they die; the consequence of both statements is that there is a time when the gods do not exist" (*Rhetoric*, 1399b, 6–8). Since one cannot conceive the non-existence of the gods, it follows that gods have neither birth nor death and are eternal. Yamakawa points out that this reasoning of Xenophanes is identical to what we find in a fragment by Parmenides:

> Only one tale is left of the way: that it is; and on this are posted many signs, that what-is is ungenerated and imperishable, a whole of one kind, unperturbed and complete. Never was it, nor shall it be, since it now *is*, all together, one, continuous. For what birth would you seek

of it? Where [or: how], whence did it grow? Not from what-is-not will I allow you to say or to think; for it is not sayable or thinkable that it is not. And what need would have stirred it later or earlier, starting from nothing, to grow? Thus it must be completely, or not at all.[23]

Again, in this inheritance of the method of indirect proof from Xenophanes, it becomes clear that, far from turning his back on the Ionian school, Parmenides actively placed himself in its lineage. Despite this, the indirect proofs essayed by Parmenides are understood to have overturned the premises of natural philosophy, because fragments like the following appear to establish the supremacy of thinking over being:

For the same thing is there for thinking and for being.
    If nothing existed, there would be nothing to think about. If being did not exist, the thought would not even exist. In fact, without being . . . you will not find thinking.[24]

This fragment has been interpreted as meaning "it is the same to think and to be." That is to say, it is a statement of idealism to the effect that thinking determines being. What Parmenides is saying, though, is the opposite. Being exists, and all thinking deals with being. When there is no coherence in thinking, it means that the object of thinking cannot be existent, as for example with Pythagoras's kenon or void.

Far from rejecting the materialist thought of the Ionians, Parmenides takes it as a premise. At one time, the natural philosophers rejected personified gods. They used reason (logos) to clear away a sensible and imaginative world of illusion. However, the illusion Parmenides sought to clear was rather one born of reason, as in Pythagoras's notion of a realm of truth that transcends the senses. For Parmenides, this realm of truth is nothing (nonexistence), and therefore an illusion. This illusion is different from that produced by the senses. Illusion produced by the senses can be rectified by reason. However, it is difficult for reason to rectify illusion born of reason. The only possibility is to demonstrate how thinking falls into self-contradiction. If we are to see something really groundbreaking in Parmenides, it is this critique of reason.

Needless to say, I have Kant in mind here. Whereas older philosophy set as its task to critique a sensibility-based illusion by way of reason, Kant sought to critique the kind of illusion (Schein) that reason itself generates. This kind of illusion is actually indispensable for reason, and therefore reason cannot easily displace it. Kant called this world of illusion "transcendental illusion." Illusion of this sort is born of reason, and by the same token reason alone can critique it. Hence what Kant means by "critique" is the critique of reason by reason itself.

I see in Parmenides a forerunner to this sense of critique. Or conversely, I see in Kant the inheritance of Parmenides. Kant made the distinction between three things: the thing in itself, phenomena, and illusion. Kant is a materialist who affirms that things reside externally. However, what we capture is not the things in themselves but a subjectively constructed phenomenon. In this case, phenomenon effectively means scientific cognition. Thus, phenomenon is different from illusion; while phenomenon is rooted in human sensible intuition, illusion is not. Further, some illusions are formed purely by reason; they are transcendental illusions. These are the most difficult to deal with and were a target of *The Critique of Pure Reason*.

The distinction Kant proposes between phenomenon and the thing in itself may appear to be another version of the dual-world theory, with its illusory world of the senses, and the true world of reason. Of course this is not the case; Kant's target was illusion, but especially the illusion of the true world. Notwithstanding, the thing in itself has been understood as the true world. This misunderstanding arises because Kant presented the thing in itself directly and actively. Kant himself was aware of the possibility of misunderstanding. After the publication of *The Critique of Pure Reason*, he wrote to a friend that he had originally conceived the work under a different plan, and it would have been better if he had stuck with it.[25]

The plan Kant first conceived was, rather than to present the distinction between phenomenon and the thing in itself from the start, to begin the work with a discussion of antinomies (the dialectic); that is to say, to begin by demonstrating that if the distinction between phenomenon and the thing in itself is not maintained, one falls into paradox, or in other words, to give an indirect proof of the existence of the thing in itself. Kant's concern was that, by omitting this step of indirect proof and launching straight into the discussion, the thing in itself might be taken for an idealistic realm that transcends the senses, and his concern proved well founded.

One needs a tripartite distinction of the form: phenomenon, thing in itself, and illusion, to understand Parmenides as well. In Parmenides's extant philosophical treatise in verse, *On Nature*, the goddess tells of the two "ways of inquiry for thinking," first "the path of Persuasion (Truth)," and second the "inscrutable track." The path of persuasive Truth consists in the recognition: "What-is is, for being is, and nothing is not." However, it does not rest there as the goddess also advises he must follow the inscrutable track. "Here I cease from faithful account and thought about truth; from this point on learn mortal opinions, hearing the deceptive order of my words."[26] But whence comes this necessity for one who knows truth to learn mortal opinions?

Mortal opinions, though, for Parmenides, do not mean illusion. In Kant's organization this would be phenomena, that is to say, thinking through the use of sensible intuitions. Aristotle, as we saw before, characterizes Parmenides as saying, "what-is is one"; however, "being forced to follow the observed facts," he proceeds to investigation of sensible reality. However, Aristotle has the sequence backward. Parmenides, by first introducing the path of Truth, cleared away any illusion of a true world that transcends the senses. With this process, he opened up the path to the investigation of phenomena.

Illusion is represented more than anything by the kind of Pythagorean thought that would reject the sensible realities and discover the origin of the world in number. What Parmenides advises is to first clear away this kind of illusion and move on to inquiry into mortal opinions (phenomena). Put another way, clear away Pythagorean philosophy, and return to the path of understanding of nature opened by the Ionian school, and proceed further down its path. And in fact the next generation of Eleatic philosophers would carry out that task—and from their effort would come the atomic theory.

....

POST-ELEATICS

Empedocles

The Eleatics are often thought to have rejected Ionian natural philosophy, but, as I have argued, they were in fact reestablishing it. In asserting the One Being, Parmenides rejected the idea of generation from nothing, and supported the permanence of the original matter. How, then, does the original matter as One take on a multiplicity of forms? Thinkers who sought to carry on the legacy of natural philosophy after the Eleatics had to solve this problem. From this a pluralism emerged.

Empedocles was the first of these pluralist thinkers. He found at the base of all things four roots: fire, air, water, and earth. It goes without saying that he owes a debt here to Ionian thinkers. For Thales, water; for Anaximenes, air; and for Heraclitus, fire. To this he added the fourth element, earth, and gave to each the name of a god. According to a fragment in Plutarch, "he calls the fervent heat and aether 'Zeus,' air 'life-giving Hera,' earth 'Aidoneus,' and the seed, as it were, and water, 'Nestis' and the mortal spring."[27] But that is not to say these were mythological ideas.

Where Empedocles differs from the Ionian school is that these four roots are mutually independent and on an equal basis. The philosophers of the Ionian school each sought to explain the variety of things from a single original substance. Sensing the problem with this line of reasoning early on, Anaximander posited behind these four forms of matter "the boundless." However, the boundless was more idea than matter. This is why he speaks of a generativity leading from the boundless to the bounded. And in this sense, his thought is related to the Pythagorean idea of a world generated from the void.

On the other hand, after Anaximander posited the boundless, his pupil Anaximenes returned to matter and identified the arche as air. In a parallel fashion, in response to Pythagoras's identification of number as the arche, Empedocles too returned to matter, reintroducing all four original forms of matter identified by the Ionians. However, he did not distinguish one as fundamental. All four were mutually equal and not reducible to a single matter nor to the boundless. They do not change into something else, nor combine to produce something new. They neither come to be from the void, nor do they pass away.

When Empedocles states the following, he follows Parmenides: "For from what in no way is, it is impossible to come to be, and for what-is to perish cannot be fulfilled or known."[28] Consequently, all things receive their form by the combination and separation of these four elements. And for Empedocles, love (philia) provides combination, and strife (neikos) separation. Love and strife here are not to be understood as psychological categories; they are rather physical forces like gravitation and repulsion. Empedocles utilized these principles of combination and separation to conceive a kind of evolution of the creatures. As discussed before, this did not involve a teleology, but rather was an evolution by natural selection. Here I would like to touch on Empedocles's understanding of social change.

Empedocles divided the evolution of society into four periods. In the first, love rules over all and the four elements (roots) exist in harmony. In the second, strife creeps in and the four elements are gradually separated and mixed. In the third age, strife alone is dominant, which is the age of division. In the fourth, love returns, and the four elements gradually begin to recombine in an age of mixture.

Described in this way, it seems clear Empedocles had in mind Hesiod's five ages (golden, silver, bronze, heroic, and iron) from the *Theogony*. Hesiod's Iron Age corresponds here to Empedocles's third age dominated by strife. And just as Hesiod discovered hope, Empedocles discerned in his system the possibility of change. This possibility he termed love.

Atomism

Following Empedocles, Anaxagoras imagined the world composed not of four elements but of a numberless amount. If, as Parmenides said, what-is cannot be born from nothing, then it is necessary to posit an infinite number of seeds for what-is. Anaxagoras says, "Coming to be and perishing the Greeks do not treat properly. For no object comes to be or perishes, but each is mixed together from and segregated into existing objects. And thus they should really call 'coming to be' mixture, and 'perishing' segregation."[29]

In Anaxagoras's thinking, the world is composed of a boundless number of seeds, each of which contains its opposite. "Everything is in everything." Melissus followed with this thought: "If there were many things, they would have to be just like I say the one is." Atomism is an extrapolation of this line of thinking.[30]

Leucippus was the first to conceive of an infinite number of identical elements, themselves not capable of further division, called atoms. He further introduced the idea of the void as the empty space in which atoms move. Leucippus was originally an Eleatic, and a pupil of Zeno. Hence, Leucippus's void follows the thought of Parmenides, for whom the void (nothing) is nonexistent. What Parmenides rejected was the Pythagorean notion that the world is generated out of the void. Leucippus, meanwhile, conceived the void as the empty space in which atoms as a fullness (*plērēs*) moved. Atoms themselves neither come into being nor perish. They rather move in empty space, and through their mutual colliding and entanglement all things come into being. In this way Leucippus was able to preserve Parmenides's thinking while accounting for a world of multiplicity, and his own pupil Democritus pushed this line of thinking forward. In Democritus's thought, coming into being and perishing result from the combination and dissociation of atoms, while transformations of substance are the result of differences in the order and direction of the atoms involved.

Empedocles thought that he could adequately explain the myriad of things by the different combinations of the four elements. By comparison, the motion of numberless indivisible bodies posited by the Atomists seems a step forward. However, Empedocles did not only posit the four basic elements. Aëtius records, "Empedocles and Xenocrates held that the elements are themselves composed of smaller bulks, those which were the most minute, and may be termed the elements of elements."[31] In other words, Empedocles conceived of the atom as a smaller building block of the four elements. Why, then, did he not proceed in the direction of an atomic theory? Seen from the point of view of atomism, Empedocles's theory would appear inconsistent. However, that is not to say Empedocles's view is invalidated by the atomic theory.

Physics has developed up to the present as an effort to identify the atom, that is, that which is itself not capable of further division. This search has moved successively from the atom named by Dalton in the nineteenth century to the subatomic particles (electron, proton, neutron) in the early twentieth century, to the stable of quarks, charms, spins, and symmetries by which we understand matter today. That is to say, what was once regarded as atomic, that is, indivisible, is itself found to be composed of particles subordinate to that. However, the discovery of an atom at a more fundamental level does not entitle one to dismiss as mere illusion what was formerly regarded as atom or element.

For example, the molecule exists as a combination of atoms; however, that does not mean that it can be reduced to the atomic level. Things possess a different character at the molecular level than at the atomic level. Regardless of how elementary a level one arrives at, one cannot ignore the particularity of the preceding levels. In this sense, while Empedocles's thesis of the four elements appears a half measure from the point of view of atomism, it could be said that he had grasped a quality that cannot be reduced to atomism.

This becomes important when we see atomic theory not just as natural philosophy but also as social philosophy. Today social atomism, that is to say the theory that would explain the social whole in terms of its component parts, is the mainstream in social philosophy. There is a critique in response to this that would stress the priority of the whole to the individual, that is to say holism. And there is further the Hegelian view that would see part and whole determined in a mutual, dialectical relation. Each of these starts from the premise of the opposition of part and whole.

In each case, the dimension where individual relates to individual drops out. The perspective of part and whole itself causes us to miss the structure that is brought about by the relation of individual to individual. As long as one is caught in this way of thinking, one cannot grasp society in its historical aspect. For example, in this book, I aim to understand social history based on four modes of exchange and their combination and separation. This is not to see society from the point of view of part and whole, but to understand social formations through the various forms in which individual and individual relate. My particular interest in the thought of Empedocles is because of this point.

From Polis to Cosmopolis

The history of Greek philosophy is generally divided into the period before and after Parmenides. However, the really substantial difference is between Empedocles and those who come after. In order to see this, one has to discern political differences. We can surmise Parmenides's radical democratic tendencies from the willingness of his pupil Zeno to wager his life on democratic reform. In the same way, Empedocles was active in efforts to reinstate isonomia.

Plutarch noted his political commitments: "Empedocles fearlessly charged the leading citizens of embezzlement, shouting 'banish them,' and alleviated damage to crops and the plague by walling off the mountain passes through which the south wind burst onto the plain."[32] It is said that he was a man of versatile talent. "Satyrus says in his *Lives* that he was both a physician and a superior orator. Gorgias of Leontini became his student, a man who excelled in oratory and left behind a treatise containing a complete system of the art. . . . Satyrus further reports that Gorgias claimed that he personally attended Empedocles' magic ceremonies, and that he professes this science."[33]

From these accounts, we see that Empedocles left behind mysterious reports. He is said, for example, to have healed a dead woman and a woman on whom the physicians had given up, that a booming voice in the middle of the night accompanied by a ray of light called him up to heaven, and that he had thrown himself into the caldera of Mount Etna in order to validate the rumor that he had become a god. Setting aside the reliability of these tales, the quantity attests to the degree Empedocles captured the imagination and respect of the people of his polis as a prophet and gives evidence that Empedocles, like Heraclitus and Parmenides, was a thinker of his polis.

However, philosophers after Empedocles and down to Democritus were no longer anchored in the polis. Nor was this a matter of individual choice. Rather it was related to the emergence of Athens after the Persian Wars as a kind of empire, and the loss by the individual poleis of both internal and external autonomy. Up until that time, thinkers mingled freely with thinkers from other poleis from a base in their own polis, but this mutual autonomy had become difficult to sustain. Instead, they went to the Greek economic and political center in Athens. Once there, of course, they were shut out from participation in the Athenian polis, that is to say, from politics. Many of them were active instead as a kind of merchant selling intellectual wares.

Because all the Ionian thinkers were descendants of original colonists and were themselves free to move, they did not attach to a particular polis simply by reason of being born there. They laid their emphasis, rather, in ensuring that the polis that they freely chose lived up to the gravity of that choice. For that, they were willing to live and die in honor and faith to their polis, and offer their life if necessary for its protection, as the legend of Zeno's resistance and death at the hands of a tyrant suggests. The thinkers we have examined till now, Heraclitus, Parmenides, Zeno, and Empedocles, were all political in this sense.

However, they lived in this manner in an age when it was still a possibility. After Athens gained hegemony in the middle of the fifth century BCE, the individual polis was autonomous in name only. Thinkers in the Ionian lineage subsequently felt the pull of the political center in Athens, but through that lost their orientation to the polis, which is to say they became apolitical. This is because, as foreigners in Athens, they had no path to citizenship. This strengthened among these expatriates a tendency toward cosmopolitanism, individualism, and the dominance of atomism. Atomism in this sense was a means of perceiving the individual in a wider space (the cosmopolis), separated from the social relations of the polis. As Democritus says, "The whole earth is open to the wise man. For a noble soul has the whole world as its native country."[34]

Conversely, this made it impossible to think in terms of the social relation of individual to individual, that is to say, to think as a member of a polis, or politically. What one can do under these circumstances is to avoid any deep investment in the current state of affairs in reality, that is to say, to become skeptical. Such was the general stance of the foreign thinkers in Athens labeled Sophists. Further, what the individual can attain is a detachment from external things, and the preservation of a calm and peaceful spirit. This kind of attitude became general in Greek thought after Athens fell under the rule of Alexander in the third century, in the form of the Stoics and the Epicureans. The Stoics affirmed in principle the need for intellectuals to participate in politics, and in fact the Lesser Cato, Seneca, and Marcus Aurelius emerged from their ranks. However, these men were fundamentally apolitical. The purpose of their philosophy was to engage in the worldly politics of empire, while maintaining a calmness of the mind untroubled by that pursuit.

Chapter 5

Socrates and Empire

....

THE ATHENIAN EMPIRE AND DEMOCRACY

In the preceding pages I have examined Greek thought from the side of the colonial cities in Ionia and the cities on the coast of southern Italy built by Ionian immigrants. Let us now take a look at the same history from the side of Athens. As we have outlined before, it is not simply that democracy came later to Athens but that Athenian democracy was under the influence of Ionian political thought from the outset. For example, the reforms of Solon (ca. 594 BCE) were an attempt to institute principles of isonomia developed in the Ionian cities. However, isonomia cannot be realized in a society with entrenched class divisions, and the reforms of Solon were blocked by the opposition of the nobility.

What crushed the opposition of the nobility in this case, violently at times, was the tyranny of Peisistratus. The usual interpretation is that Athenian democracy begins with the termination of the tyrant system and the reforms of Cleisthenes in 508 BCE. However, we must pay attention to the connection between democracy and the reign of the tyrant. It is true that democracy begins with the overthrow of the tyrannical system; however, the relation between the two is not as simple as it may appear. For example, in suppressing the resistance of the aristocratic class, the tyrant Peisistratus was hailed by the nonlanded majority. If democracy is rule of the majority, this rule was realized under the system of tyranny.

Of course, strictly speaking, democracy is established on the removal of the tyrant. However, democracy is not possible without the preceding period of tyranny. Moreover, democracy is by no means isonomia (no-rule), but another form of rule (-cracy). It was well understood by those who brought down the tyrant that majority rule harbors within it the possibility of producing another tyrant. The reforms of Cleisthenes demonstrate understanding and had a variety of defenses built in to avoid the reemergence of the tyrant system.

First, the duties of public office were usually chosen by lot. This prevented administrative monopolization of power. However, the lottery system was utterly inappropriate for selecting generals. To leave war to an incompetent general was to risk losing everything. However, it is difficult to avoid an accomplished general garnering popularity among the masses. Against this, multiple commanders were appointed at the same time in order to avoid a monopoly on distinction for military deeds, and then the record of generals was closely scrutinized. Notwithstanding, they were not able to avoid the emergence into administration of figures of distinction. What was employed at this point was the system of ostracism. Here pottery fragments were used for an anonymous system of voting, and powerful individuals who it was feared might later appear as tyrants could be exiled for a period of ten (later relaxed to five) years.

This kind of system was proposed to avoid democracy reverting back into tyranny. Notwithstanding, it was unable to prevent this reversion. Though not tyranny as such, an endless series of demagogues emerged. And then with the defeat of Athens in the Peloponnesian War (431–4 BCE), as with the Thirty Tyrants, despotic rule by oligarchy emerged. Why was this unavoidable? It is because at the root of democracy there is the tyrant system. This is why when democracy (rule by the many) is endangered, tyranny often emerges.

Next, the fact that the demagogues and the Thirty Tyrants appeared at the time of the Peloponnesian War indicates that democracy cannot be just a matter of a single state. The process by which democracy was established in Athens cannot be severed from the process by which Athens imposed its rule (-cracy) over the other poleis. Let us take a look at this process in the context of the relations of Athens and the Ionian city-states.

When the Ionian states jointly planned a rebellion against Persia, they sought support from the contemporary military power, Athens. However, in part because Athens could not sufficiently answer that call, they met with a disastrous defeat. Athens subsequently entered into an all-out war with the Persians, and as a result of that victory were able to set free the occupied Ionian states. Athens further became leader of the Delian League, in resistance to the Persians, a league with nearly two hundred signatory states. This arrangement was called a league; however, in reality this was a form of empire in which Athens levied taxes and exerted rule over the other states.

As time went on, the estrangement of the other city-states from Athens and subsequent suppression produced continual conflict, which ended with the outbreak of the Peloponnesian War between Athens and an anti-Athenian confederation led by Sparta. Athens's defeat in this war in 404 BCE ended the Athenian empire, and signaled that the zenith of Athenian political, economic, and cultural influence had passed.

Looking back on these events, the rise of Athenian democracy occurred during the time of its victory in the Persian War and the ascent of Pericles to leadership, but this was also the period of Athens's rise as an empire. It was Pericles who enacted the statutes that denied citizenship to foreign-born residents. Until that point, no small number of foreigners had been able to become Athenian citizens, but from that point on Athens became an exclusive community. This point is inextricably tied to Athens's rule over other poleis and exploitation of foreigners residing in Athens.

Hannah Arendt draws a distinction between empire and imperialism, which will allow a set of points to be made here with respect to the Athenian empire. An empire possesses a principle by which to rule over diverse people, whereas imperialism is the mere expansion of a nation-state or polis. For example, Napoleon's aim to rule over a European empire was a simple imperialist extension of the nation-state in the absence of any principle for rule. This has the paradoxical effect of sharpening the nationalist consciousnesses of the diverse people under that rule.[1]

Arendt, of course, understood imperialism as a problem of the modern capitalist state; however, her conception is applicable to Athens in the age of Pericles. In the evolving Athenian state, emphasis was placed on the exclusion of those outside a strict lineage based on territorial bonds. This conception transcended the blood relations of tribal society and in a sense constituted the formation of a nation.

Because of this exclusivity, however, as Athens expanded its territory and brought other poleis under its control, it could only take the form of imperialism, because it possessed no principle under which to form an empire. By contrast, Persia was an empire. The Persians subjugated the various countries within their empire; however, aside from certain set forms of submission and tribute, they allowed a good deal of autonomy in their internal affairs. Further, the Persians had the apparatus of the bureaucracy and a standing army. The Athenians, though, while expanding the territory under their control through their victory over the Persians, were not able to execute an empire of this sort.

Until Athens seized hegemony, the Greek poleis, though constantly at war, had existed as a loose confederation, as exemplified by the Olympic Games in honor of the god Zeus. All poleis were equal in principle. If one polis should act in that context as ruler of another, it could only be imperialistic, thereby inevitably inviting a backlash from the other polis. The end result of this was the Peloponnesian War.

Of course Sparta, who was victorious in this war, and Thebes, who seized hegemony afterward, were unable to unify Greece as a whole. Sparta from the start took a hard militaristic line because of their experience with the revolts by the Messenian helots (enslaved populations). And in fact, when the Messenians achieved independence, it signaled the end of the line for Sparta.

Consequently, no empire emerged internally from Greece. It would not be until the Macedonian king Alexander that the Greek world would be unified as an empire. This period is said to be Hellenism (becoming Greek); however, the principle of this kind of empire was derived not from Greece but from Asia. As a matter of fact, when Alexander took Egypt under his rule in place of the Persians, he was welcomed as a pharaoh.

When one takes these points into consideration, it becomes clear that the form of democracy in Athens was closely connected to changes in the relation to the other poleis, to foreigners, and so forth. Pericles, for example, diverted the taxes from the various states in the Delian League and distributed them to Athenian citizens as per diem for attendance in assembly. That is to say, Athenian direct democracy was dependent upon the ruling and plundering of the other poleis. It is precisely this imperialistic expansion that was the condition of Athenian democracy. This is why it was the democratic faction that was bellicose with respect to the other poleis, and the aristocratic faction, rather, that wished to retain the customary relations of mutual respect. Even amid the maelstrom of the Peloponnesian War, the aristocrats continually sought peace.[2]

Democracy in Athens was also closely tied to the development of the slave system. With the reforms of Solon, Athenian citizens were able to escape the bonded servitude that had arisen; however, slavery remained indispensable to the system of democracy. The Athenian army was based on the mass tactics of the phalanx using a heavily armed citizen militia called hoplites. The success of these tactics provided the basis of the ascent of the democratic faction versus the aristocracy. During the Persian War in particular, the contribution of the lower class of citizens, who volunteered to row in the galleys of the warships, gained them a political position. Democracy was established as a result. However, insofar as citizens were busy with agricultural labor, they could not attend the assembly, nor could they go to war. Because of this, in order to be a fully vested Athenian citizen, it was necessary to have slaves. The citizens of Athens not only employed slaves to work in their fields, they lent them out to the silver mines for their own profit. Hence, the rise of direct democracy in Athens is inseparable from the development of a system of slave labor.

Further, following Athens's political and military ascent, it became the center of trade in the Mediterranean as well. In this it took the place of former centers in Miletus and other Ionian cities. However, the Athenian citizens themselves did not engage in commerce. They left this role to foreigners, whom they then taxed. Whatever economic contribution a foreigner might make to the polis, there was no path to citizenship, nor legal protection under the law.[3] In this way Athenian democracy was built on the exploitation of foreigners, slaves, and other poleis.

SOPHISTS AND RULE BY RHETORIC

In tandem with the establishment of democracy, Athens became a society that emphasized oratory. The idea took root that rule is exercised, not by force of arms, nor through religion and magic, but by the power of the word (logos). Of course this only applied to relations within the polis. Nor was it the case that force and magic simply disappeared. However, whether at the assembly or the court (Heliaia), when the transaction of public affairs came to be based in debate and rhetoric, the need arose among citizens to learn rhetorical technique. Hence, citizens of means had their children study it. A question remains largely unasked in relation to this rise of rhetoric in Athenian public life, though. Why is it that its instructors were largely foreigners?

The Athens of this period is regarded as the most advanced polis in terms of politics and culture. If that is the case, why would the city turn largely to foreigners to teach the arts of rhetoric and oratory? This is an indication that, while Athens was politically and economically dominant, in matters of speech and thought it was poorly developed, and the people of Athens had to learn these arts from immigrants from Ionia or the colonies established by Ionian settlers on the southern coast of Italy.[4]

In the Platonic dialogue *Gorgias*, rhetoric is portrayed as the art of persuading other people, and thereby ruling them, and the teachers of this art were the Sophists. However, the reduction of rhetoric to a set of techniques for domination was the view, not of the Sophists, but of the Athenians. The Athenians had no desire to learn anything from foreigners beyond this instrumental art of rhetoric.

It is under democracy (majority rule) that rhetoric becomes a means of ruling over other people. However, this was not the case in Ionia, where the arts of rhetoric were developed. Whether in the court or the assembly, rhetoric here also was indispensable; however, in Ionia this took the form of a means of collective inquiry (elenchos). This is the means of inquiry on which natural philosophy too was based.

As noted before, the technique of indirect proof taken as a unique practice of the Eleatics can already be found in Milesian thinkers. That is to say, rhetoric was not a set of techniques for ruling over other people, but a method for understanding a nature that included humans. The Athenians, by contrast, were uninterested in the development of the practical arts and understanding of nature. What was considered important in Athens was the technique of persuading and thereby subjugating the other in the public sphere, that is to say, the techniques of rhetoric as a means of human control. Here the strategies of argumentation of the Eleatics were employed as a means to refute and make sport of one's adversary.

Moreover, foreign residents in Athens did not teach anything beyond technique. Foreigners were prohibited from activity as citizens (public affairs), and participation in internal politics of the polis was dangerous. They were presumably well aware that Pericles's friend Anaxagoras was accused of blasphemy for asserting that the sun was a burning stone. This incident was possibly a political conspiracy against Pericles; however, the danger of foreign thinkers being suppressed on that kind of pretext was clear. What they did end up expressing, as with Protagoras, were at best skeptical and relativist opinions.

For example, we find in the dialogue *Protagoras*: "Hippias the sage spoke next. He said: All of you who are here present I reckon to be kinsmen and friends and fellow-citizens, by nature [physis] and not by law [nomos]; for by nature like is akin to like, whereas law is the tyrant of mankind, and often compels us to do many things which are against nature."[5]

Slavery and imperialism are against nature. This is the type of natural law intrinsic to Ionian natural philosophy. The same could have been said whether by Protagoras or Gorgias. In the context of Athenian imperialism, though, this is clearly a dangerous thought, so the Sophists did not openly advocate this kind of opinion. Rather, they chiefly taught practical knowledge in the form of the rhetorical arts. As a result, while regarded as useful, foreign thinkers were scorned as mere technicians.

Socrates was impeached under the following charge: "Socrates is guilty, inasmuch as he does not believe in the Gods whom the city worships, but introduces other strange deities; he is also guilty, inasmuch as he corrupts the young men, and the punishment he has incurred is death."[6] As a result, Socrates was labeled a sophist. But the real Sophists, who were foreigners resident in Athens, would have avoided placing themselves in such a compromising position or intervening in Athenian politics and customs. Consequently, what they said was unlikely to have really influenced Athenian citizens. It was rather the Athenians who used their discourse for their own convenience.

In the *Statesman*, Plato charges that, rather than merely learning from Sophists, the Athenian statesmen were themselves the greatest sophists. Again in *Gorgias*, while subjecting the representative Sophist Gorgias to scrutiny, Plato portrays him as a modest and unassuming individual. And that may well have been the case. The one who rattles on with sophistic arguments is rather the Athenian youth Callicles.

Callicles argues in the haughtiest manner for "the right of the strong and superior." Nature (physis) is the province of natural talent, action, and the will to power, while nomos, in the form of law, religion, and morality, is little more than a device for the weak to rule over the strong.[7] This is the exact reverse of the distinction the Sophist Hippias draws between physis and nomos.

Callicles's opinion reflects the strengthening of an imperialistic tendency in Athens. The seizure of power within Athens through the arts of oratory, or the trampling of other poleis by military power, constitutes nature (physis), whereas the laws, religion, and morality that suppress this are nothing more than nomos. That is to say, the characters in whose mouths opinions about realpolitik and the rights of the superior are placed are not the foreign-born Sophists, but the children of the ruling class who learned the techniques of rhetoric at their feet. This is why Plato calls the people who claim the Sophists are poisoning the youth of Athens "the greatest of all Sophists."[8]

Representative of these youths is Pericles's own close kin Alcibiades. Alcibiades was a prototypical demagogue who earned the applause of the masses with bellicose, imperialistic rhetoric. Alcibiades instigated the Sicilian expedition and was chosen as general, was accused of blasphemy in the mutilation of a statue of Hermes, and was ordered afterward to return to Athens. Rather than stand trial, he exiled himself to hostile Sparta and made a significant contribution in the campaign against Athens, and then returned—an individual altogether against convention.

Alcibiades was one of the beloved students of Socrates. It is said that this was one of the reasons for Socrates's eventual prosecution. This was the meaning of "corrupting the youth." The emergence of youths like Alcibiades, though, was not because of Socrates. And it was certainly not because of the Sophists. Nobody taught these youths to act as they did. A character like Alcibiades was rather a product of the corruption of Athenian society itself by an imperialist expansionism.

THE TRIAL OF SOCRATES

Let us recount the sequence of facts leading up to the trial of Socrates in Athens. The Peloponnesian War between the Athenian empire and the league led by Sparta stretched on for years from its inception in 431 BCE, but Sparta had on numerous occasions made bids for peace. Athens repeatedly dashed these hopes and continued the war. Prowar demagogues like Cleon, and later Alcibiades, gained the support of the people and led Athens to the brink of destruction. In 411 BCE, with signs of collapse all around, Athens established a system of rule of the four hundred. This was essentially rule by a minority (oligarchy) in which absolute power was ceded to an assembly of four hundred citizens of the upper strata. Democratic government was reestablished inside of a year; however, with the final surrender of Athens in 404 BCE, a second oligarchy was established under the supervision of the Spartan army. Known as the Thirty Tyrants, they instituted a ruthless reign of terror involving the execution and exile of many prominent members of the prowar democratic faction. Members of the faction who fled or were exiled, though, regrouped outside the state and reinstituted a democracy within a year through an accord between the oligarchs and democratic factions. However, as a result of a general amnesty included in the reconciliation agreement, supporters of the Thirty Tyrants and traitors who gave aid to the Spartans were able to escape with no inquiry into their responsibility.

The charges brought against Socrates occurred under the subsequent democratic government established in 403 BCE. Anytus was Socrates's formal accuser; however, in the background lay the prior decades of Athenian political history. The real target of the impeachment was Critias, first among the Thirty Tyrants; however, because of the terms of the reconciliation this was not possible. Socrates, then, teacher of Alcibiades and Critias, was charged in their place. Socrates himself steadfastly refused cooperation with the Thirty Tyrants. Further, the majority of Socrates's loyal followers, members of the democratic faction, were in exile. It becomes clear then, that the impeachment of Socrates was a political plot. Diogenes Laërtius writes as follows:

> He was a man of great firmness of mind, and very much attached to the democracy, as was plain from his not submitting to Critias, when he ordered him to bring Leon of Salamis, a very rich man, before the thirty, for the purpose of being murdered. And he alone voted for the acquittal of the ten generals (charged in the disastrous aftermath of the battle of Arginusae in 406 BCE); and when it was in his power to escape out of prison he would not do it; and he reproved those who bewailed his fate, and even while in prison, he delivered those beautiful discourses which we still possess.[9]

However, one would not characterize Socrates as a democrat. He cast the lone dissenting vote for acquittal precisely when the democratic faction was in power. Nor, of course, was he an aristocrat. He refused the order of Critias's men, who represented the aristocratic faction. And of course in the end it would be the democrats who impeached Socrates and found him guilty. What Socrates said and did was a mystery to both democrats and aristocrats alike. The greatest enigma, of course, was why Socrates made no attempt to evade a trial that was clearly a political trap, or his subsequent sentence of death.

This was first of all a mystery to Socrates's contemporaries. It was this mystery that inspired not just Plato and Xenophon but many writers of so-called Socratic literature. All these writers assert that Socrates was charged for a crime that had no basis. In fact, since it was later determined that the charges against Socrates were false, the accusers were themselves sanctioned. However, this did not solve the riddle. Just what kind of person was Socrates? A philosopher who did not leave behind a single work. A robust man who was dispatched to the Peloponnesian front three times and rendered distinguished service, yet staunchly advocated for peace. The riddle of this historical Socrates only deepened after his death.

At the time, those who advocated for Socrates sought to distinguish him from the Sophists, because he was being impeached as a Sophist. For example, Socrates accepted no fees for his teaching. Therefore, the argument went, he was not a Sophist. If one accepts the definition of a Sophist as one who teaches the arts of rhetoric for money, then clearly Socrates was not a Sophist. Yet, despite the fact that Socrates accepted no fees for his teaching, he was still seen by his peers as a typical Sophist. The Socrates who appears in Aristophanes's *The Clouds* (ca. 423 BCE) would at the time have been around forty-five years of age, but there can be no doubt, from the fact that he appears as the object of satire in contemporary comedy, that he was famed at the time as a Sophist.

In this play, a Sophist means first and foremost a person who teaches the art of "turning the inferior argument into the winning argument." Strepsiades, the protagonist of *The Clouds*, enrolls in Socrates's school for that purpose, specifically to learn how to advocate to avoid paying his debts. Socrates subjects Strepsiades to a series of seemingly absurd intellectual tasks but accepts no fee. Hence, the fact that one accepts no fee was not at the time sufficient to escape the mark of the Sophist. Second, a Sophist indicates someone who rejects the gods of the city, destroys conventional morality, and corrupts the youth. The Socrates of this play seems to be fascinated by natural philosophy, in particular the arguments of Anaximenes, who regarded air as the arche. He explains rain, thunder, lightning, and other phenomena thought heretofore to be an act of Zeus as an effect of the movement of clouds. Aristophanes's satire, then, is to say it is precisely clouds that become the gods of the new age, and the deity of those who spread their knowledge around without working, that is, the Sophists.

The actual charges lodged against Socrates were little changed from the popular conception above. They can be summarized as follows. First, Socrates did not pay due respect to the gods recognized by the polis. Second, he introduced new gods, the daimones. And third, he corrupted the youth of the polis. These suspicions were not without basis. Xenophon, for example, advocates for Socrates by saying he faithfully observed the Athenian customary rituals. However, this does not mean that he was not a Sophist. The foreigners labeled as Sophists took pains to avoid suspicion of rejecting the Athenian gods and customary morality or of corrupting the youth. Socrates, as an Athenian citizen, took no such care. If these were indeed the traits of a Sophist, then Socrates in particular merited the name. That is why he was taken up as the target of comedy. The suspicion that Socrates introduced new gods was also not without foundation. As we will outline later, he stated publicly that he acted in accord with signs from a spirit (daimon).

However, the reason Socrates appeared in the eyes of the populace as the greatest provocation to Athenian social norms was not because of the reasons listed in the formal charges. The most fundamental reason was that, in the context of Athens, he rejected the value of public life and office. According to Socrates, the daimon opposed his participation in the deeds of the state. "For the truth is, that no man who goes to war with you or any other multitude, honestly striving against the many lawless and unrighteous deeds which are done in a state, will save his life; he who will fight for the right, if he would live even for a brief space, must have a private station and not a public one."[10]

A sign from the gods of this sort was unheard of in the context of Athens, where the title of citizen was synonymous with participation in public affairs and the state. One's actions in public office determined all other affairs. The private station was by definition apolitical. Consequently, those excluded from public office, such as foreigners, women, and slaves, could only be nonpolitical, that is, nonentities in terms of the polis. Virtue in Athens was political ability, that is to say, the ability to skillfully manipulate words (logos) in the public sphere. For this reason the wealthy educated their sons in the arts of oratory from the Sophists. Socrates, however, was uninterested. "What return shall be made to the man who has never had the wit to be idle during his whole life; but has been careless of what the many care for—wealth, and family interests, and military offices, and speaking in the assembly, and magistracies, and plots, and parties."[11]

This is not to be interpreted as indifference to public matters or the question of right. Nor was Socrates's insistence on his private status because he could not "live even for a brief space" if acting in a public capacity. As he demonstrated in his actions at the Peloponnesian front, and in his final acceptance of the sentence of the Athenians, he certainly did not fear death. Moreover, communications from the daimon forbade Socrates certain things, but never offered a reason. The daimon did not forbid Socrates to fight for what he considered right, but rather only to do so in a public capacity. This prohibition by the gods further implied that truly just action cannot be carried out from a public station. In following this order, Socrates rejected the generally recognized values of the Athenians, which held one's deeds in public office and one's political actions to be the foundation of virtue.

Unlike the Sophists, who accepted fees to teach the arts of rhetoric, Socrates accepted no fee. This was neither because he was wealthy nor because he was sympathetic with the accusation that receiving compensation was a prostitution of knowledge. It was because from the start he was not teaching an instrumental art, thus was not in a position to demand fees. The arts of rhetoric the noncitizen Sophists taught were necessary in order to participate actively in the assembly and in the courts. That is, they had use value. To receive consideration for that was a legitimate exchange.

Socrates recognized no value in participation in the assembly and courts and the attainment of power. The art he taught was not for the purpose of action in the public sphere; rather, it was a means of severing one's ties to it. "Corruption of the youth" refers precisely to this. The Sophists, on the contrary, did nothing to overturn the common sense of the Athenian citizen, who placed great value in the acquisition of power in the public sphere. Consequently, what was indecipherable to the Athenian citizen, whether for or against Socrates, was the reason for this behavior.

THE RIDDLE OF SOCRATES

The riddle of Socrates lay in this stance of fighting for truth and justice, not from a public position but from a private one. This was a contradiction, because to be in the private sphere was to be apolitical. Socrates lived this paradox, and it rendered both his life and his death enigmatic. The images of Socrates fostered and cherished by his pupils after his death were redolent with this sense of enigma.

One aspect of this image can be found in the writing of Plato and Aristotle, to whom we might add Xenophon as well. This would be the legacy of Socrates's commitment to the polis. A second aspect is found in the writings of his longtime follower Antisthenes, regarded as founder of the Cynics, and Antisthenes's pupil Diogenes and his circle. This would be the inheritance of Socrates's stance of rejecting public action. We might call the former lineage the major Socratics and the latter the minor Socratics. Because of the enormous influence of Plato's works, in most of which Socrates appears as a character, it is generally thought that Socrates must have been much like the kind of person described by Plato. However, the historical Socrates would appear to have more closely resembled the image of the minor Socratics.

What Socrates brought about was an inversion of the value associated with public and private capacity. This was first of all to place the private in a position of superiority to the public, hence political. The set of his disciples known as the Cynics accomplished this inversion. Diogenes, who was a foreigner, had no need to go to the trouble of abandoning public life. To those denied a path to public life, it was already a dog's existence. However, Diogenes did not merely content himself with his position as a dog. According to Diogenes Laërtius's *Lives of the Philosophers*, he obliged those who treated him like a dog by actually behaving like a dog, going around and marking his territory and so forth. He was a beggar and lived in a tub by the side of the road.

In scandalously rejecting the value of public affairs and the polis in this thorough equation of the private with the doglike, the Cynics formed an opposition to Plato and his followers, with their aspirations to public life. Further, in a period when the polis was losing its independence, they were able to exemplify to people a way to live. In reply to someone who asked where he was a citizen, Diogenes is reported to have replied, "I am a citizen of the world [the cosmopolis]."

Cynicism gained in popularity during the period when the Greek city-states fell under the reign of Alexander's empire. According to Diogenes Laërtius, when Alexander the Great stood in front of him and asked him what he desired, Diogenes replied, "I'd like you to stop standing in front of me and blocking the sun." However, the period when the Cynics were able to mount some effective resistance was when there was still some memory of the prosperous days of the polis. As the poleis became more and more powerless under the rule of empire, both the Cynics and the followers of Plato were rendered impotent. In later years Epicurus and Zeno and the Stoics would appear to inherit the legacy of the Cynics. However, they no longer displayed the provocative character of the Cynics. In an age when the Greek polis had been reduced to an administrative unit in the empire, Epicurus and the Stoics developed a philosophy of individualism that aimed to live under empire according to an indifference.

By contrast, Plato and Xenophon were Athenian citizens who regarded the importance of active participation in public affairs to be self-evident. They took, then, Socrates's teachings as a guide to the conduct of politicians within the state. After Socrates's death, Plato thoroughly pursued one aspect of Socrates, that is to say, the idea that one must contribute to the life of the polis, in whatever form. Plato sought the origin of his thinking about idealism, the philosopher-king, and so forth in the Socrates he created. However, one cannot therefore label this a complete misinterpretation. Socrates would never become a public figure; however, neither would he rest content merely with the private. He did remain a private figure within the polis; however, never did he neglect to continue to truly fight for the right. Plato sought the true form of the polity rooted in this Socrates.

Socrates's position, however, was identical to neither those of Diogenes nor Plato. Socrates's position can be boiled down to this: act publicly while remaining in your private station, which is to say, while remaining within the polis, be cosmopolitan. From this perspective, Socrates seems more political than the Cynics, while being cosmopolitan in comparison to Plato.

To understand the inversion of values brought about by Socrates, it is illuminating to refer to Kant in *What Is Enlightenment?* For Kant, to act in accord with the position of the state is the private, while the universal standpoint (of the citizen of the world) is the public. To truly be public, one must take up a private station that transcends the state. Of course, such a cosmopolis transcending the state as such does not exist. What Kant is saying is that while existing as an individual within the state, one should make judgments and act as a citizen of the world. That is to say, Kant's inversion of value between public and private is neither Plato's nor Diogenes's, but rather Socrates's position.

A second point of reference is the early Marx's *Contribution to the Critique of Hegel's Philosophy of Right*. Hegel placed the state atop civil society. Civil society here is conceived as a system of desires, while the state transcends this at the rational level. That is to say, in civil society people function in a private capacity, while in the state they become public citizens; that is to say, they assume their true form. Marx inverted this proposition. If people exhibit their real form in a private capacity, there is no need to assume a public sphere. To put it in Marx's terms, if people exhibit their "species-being" in civil society, there is no longer any need for the political state above that. That is to say, if one can dissolve the class antagonisms within civil society, the state as a political entity will be superseded.[12]

Let us consider this set of issues in the context of Athens. There was direct democracy in Athens. However, this is not something that transcended the division between civil society and the political state. Civil society in Athens was riven by deep class conflict, and the majority of citizens were poor. Democracy in Athens meant the seizure of power by the majority and the redistribution of wealth through taxation of the nobility and the wealthiest members. As one would expect, this was met with resistance by the nobility and the elite. This kind of conflict does not admit of a solution. This is because it seeks to resolve the problem by redistribution of wealth without addressing the reason for the gaps between rich and poor in civil society, and the social conditions by which it is given rise. What gives the appearance of solving this internal class antagonism is the imperialistic policies that seek a source of wealth in the exploitation of foreign countries. And what instigates this strategy and gains its popular assent is the demagogue.

To be active in Athens as a public figure entailed aiming to capture the support of the majority in order to gain power. Even in direct democracy, ultimately, the leaders spoke on behalf of the people. And from this situation was born a ceaseless parade of demagoguery. In response to this, Socrates declined to become a public figure. How, then, did he seek to change Athenian society? Socrates himself had no positive agenda. However, he ceaselessly cast doubt on the public/private distinction and the values self-evident to Athenians at the time.

For example, Socrates placed state affairs and domestic affairs, that is to say the public and political and the private and economic, on the same footing. These are Socrates's words, according to Xenophon in the *Memorabilia*:

Don't look down on business men, Nicomachides. For the management of private concerns differs only in point of number from that of public affairs. In other respects they are much alike, and particularly in this, that neither can be carried on without men, and the men employed in private and public transactions are the same. For those who take charge of public affairs employ just the same men when they attend to their own; and those who understand how to employ them are successful directors of public and private concerns, and those who do not, fail in both.[13]

Socrates continues, "If you succeed with one [household], you can set to work on a larger number. But if you can't do anything for one, how are you going to succeed with many?"[14] We find here no distinction between the virtue of a private person and the virtue of a public figure. He made no distinction between freeman and slave. For example, in response to Eutherus, whose household had fallen into poverty because of the loss of land in the colonies and the need to support many free relatives, Socrates asked if he should not place himself in the service of others. When Eutherus expresses reservations about "making himself a slave," Socrates continues, "But surely those who control their cities and take charge of public affairs are thought more respectable, not more slavish on that account."[15]

In this way Socrates rejects the distinction between public and private, as well as the hierarchies of status to which it is tied. It is said that Socrates was the first to inquire into the basis of ethics. However, this only means that he discovered virtue in a space that transcends the distinction between public action and private action. This further hints at a civil society where there is no split between one's public and private lives. This vision of Socrates, though, was not an idle dream. This was an actually existing society in Ionia. And its principle was isonomia. In Athens, by contrast, one's status and actions as a public figure were what chiefly counted, and labor, in both domestic and commercial spheres, was held in contempt.[16]

DAIMON

Neither those who accused Socrates nor those who supported him really understood what Socrates was thinking. This was largely because Socrates himself did not fully understand it. Socrates's claim was that he behaved as he did in obedience to "signs from the gods [*kaina daimonia*]." He received as well instruction from oracles and dreams. Further, he made no effort to conceal these signs and voices, and publicly declared them in court:

> Some may wonder why I go about in private giving advice and busying myself with the concerns of others, but do not venture to come forward in public and advise the state. I will tell you why. You have heard me speak at sundry times and in diverse places of an oracle or sign which Meletus ridicules in the indictment. This sign, which is a kind of voice, first began to come to me when I was a child; it always forbids but never commands me to do anything which I am going to do. This voice, in response to my participation in the affairs of the state, tells me no.[17]

We may take the *Apology*, in contrast to the other Platonic dialogues, to be based in the actual words of Socrates. The courtroom was packed with the citizens of Athens; hence Plato was not in a position to take liberties with Socrates's defense. In particular the above statements constitute a recognition by Socrates of one of the principle charges against him, that he introduced new gods to Athens, so we can expect that he spoke largely as it is presented here.

Socrates is presented in Aristophanes's *The Clouds* as the kind of person who would respond to the naive invocation of the name of Zeus by the protagonist with, "That stinks of the age of Kronos! What a primitive sense."[18] So, when Socrates mentions the daimon, is he really, as in the charges against him, introducing new gods in place of the gods of Olympus? In fact, the daimon belongs to a much greater antiquity than Zeus and the personified gods of Olympus, with truly a primeval sense. It is this god rather that would have felt familiar to the townspeople of Athens. Socrates also was subject to the oracles of Apollo, but this too would have been close to the sensibilities of the average Greek. In this sense, one cannot say that Socrates was introducing strange new gods.

Socrates's own words show that he had the gift of receiving signs from a supernatural entity like the daimon. But that kind of capacity was not unusual at the time. What was particular about Socrates was not the fact of communication from the daimon, but the content of the message. And what was most significant was the proscription by the daimon against activity in the public sphere. So, what was the daimon? Hegel, for example, argues that "we would be mistaken to think of this as a spirit or guardian angel, nor can we simply think of it as the activity of conscience."

Since everyone here has this personal mind which appears to him to be his mind, we see how in connection with this, we have what is known under the name of the Genius [*daimonion*] of Socrates; for it implies that now man decides in accordance with his perception and by himself. But in this Genius of Socrates—notorious as a much discussed *bizarrerie* of his imagination—we are neither to imagine the existence of protective spirit, angel, and such-like, nor even of conscience. For conscience is the idea of universal individuality, of the mind certain of itself, which is at the same time universal truth. But the Genius of Socrates is rather all the other and necessary sides of his universality, that is, the individuality of mind which came to consciousness in him equally with the former. His pure consciousness stands over both sides. The deficiency in the universal, which lies in its indeterminateness, is unsatisfactorily supplied in an individual way, because Socrates' judgment, as coming from himself, was characterized by the form of an unconscious impulse. The Genius of Socrates is not Socrates himself, not his opinions and conviction, but an oracle which, however, is not external, but is subjective, his oracle. It bore the form of a knowledge which was directly associated with a condition of unconsciousness; it was a knowledge which may also appear under other conditions as a magnetic state. It may happen that at death, in illness and catalepsy, men know about circumstances future or present, which, in the understood relations of things, are altogether unknown. These are facts which are usually rudely denied. That in Socrates we should discover what we expect comes to pass through conscious reflection in the form of the unconscious [makes it seem exceptional].[19]

For Hegel, we discover in Socrates what we would "expect to come to pass through conscious reflection, in the form of the unconscious," or the daimon. That is to say, Socrates could only become aware of his own decisions in the form of signs from the daimon. However, we should not take this to mean that Socrates was lacking in understanding. Nor was this a question of his talents or personal inclination. What is crucial here is that the thought at which Socrates arrives can in no way be grasped through conscious reflection.

The messages from the daimon forbade Socrates to act in a public capacity. However, this did not mean a withdrawal from the polis and the world of affairs, but rather a command to act on their behalf in a private capacity. This sign from the daimon is consistent with a command to make the polis a space where there is no distinction between public and private. But as we have discussed, such a society, lacking a distinction between public and private, already existed in Ionia. This was isonomia. But such a society was not only lost with the fall of Ionia, it was erased from memory, except that it lived on in faint traces in the stream of Ionian natural philosophy.

Socrates himself would not have been aware of this. It is said that he studied the Ionian philosophers earnestly in his youth, but eventually turned to questions of ethics and the soul not found in the Ionians. However, it was rather when Socrates separated himself from inquiry into nature in the narrow sense that he inherited what lay at the root of Ionian natural philosophy. Of course this was not a matter he arrived at through conscious reflection, but rather through signs from the daimon. Socrates did not appear to have any idea why these communications came to him. Yet he felt compelled to obey them.

My sense is that what appeared to Socrates in the form of signs from the daimon was the return of the repressed. The object of repression was, without doubt, the form of isonomia that characterized Ionian society, that is to say, mode of exchange D. Consequently, this could not be brought to the form of conscious reflection. For Socrates this was a compulsion. In this peculiar individual, the source of Ionian philosophy made a return.

THE SOCRATIC METHOD

In Athenian society, the struggles between the aristocratic and democratic factions became a feature of life. This took a particularly virulent form during the years of the Peloponnesian War, and Socrates affiliated himself with neither camp. Both camps did have certain values in common—specifically, that labor was the business of slaves, while the imperative for the citizen was action in public affairs and the acquisition of political power. In this sense virtue indicates talent in public affairs. This shared premise, however, was exactly what Socrates called into question.

So, what is one to do? If one wants to bring about changes in the system of society, that means attending the assembly and using one's persuasive powers to move people to action. That is to say, it means functioning as a public person. However, the daimon closed off this path. In fact, this was not sufficient to change the premise of Athenian society.

The path Socrates chose was to go to the agora (the public square or marketplace), call out to whichever citizen passed by, and engage him in a dialogue. "[I] am a sort of gadfly, given to the state by God; and the state is a great and noble steed who is tardy in his motions owing to his very size, and requires to be stirred into life. I am that gadfly which God has attached to the state, and all day long and in all places am always fastening upon you, arousing and persuading and reproaching you."[20]

The first point to which to attend is that Socrates proceeded not to the assembly but to the public square. In the public square were mixed people who had no chance of participating in public affairs: foreigners, women, slaves. If democracy was operative in the assembly, it was isonomia in the agora. That is to say, in Athens, isonomia was only possible in the agora. Hence, by limiting his activities chiefly to the agora, without consciously realizing it Socrates reinstated an Ionian style of thought.

The second point is that Socrates adopted a method, the one-on-one dialogue, that was not the method of public discourse until that time. It was likely that crowds of people gathered around to hear these dialogues. However, Socrates never turns to address the crowd itself. That is because, in the context of the dialogue, Socrates only asked questions and said nothing positive in itself. Hence, however many people gathered to hear, Socrates in the end could only interact person to person.

The Socratic method is now well known. Socrates did not, in the face of his interlocutor's assertions, argue the counterproposition. What he did, rather, was to provisionally accept his interlocutor's proposition and demonstrate that its antithesis can be drawn from it. This is what gives the Socratic dialogue its peculiar qualities. Socrates drew a connection between this method and the work of his mother, and called it a form of midwifery. He did not teach; he rather helped people realize the truth by themselves.

Socrates, however, did not originate this method. It rather follows the methods of argumentation of the Eleatics. Parmenides and Zeno sought to refute the dual world of the Pythagoreans, in which a transcendental world of truth was opposed to a transient world of illusion. They set about the task by demonstrating indirectly that, if one accepts these premises, one falls into contradiction. Socrates proceeded by the same method in Athens. However, what Socrates sought to reject through indirect proof lay in the premise, self-evident to Athenian society, of the dual world that divided the public and the private person.

What Socrates opened up was a form of virtue that transcended the distinction between public and private, between freeman and slave. This virtue was not the kind of knowledge or technique that can be taught from the outside. It can only be grasped as each individual awakens to a self that is neither public nor private. Consequently, this can only be transmitted through the encounter of person to person. Socrates had nothing positive to teach. Still, left to their own devices, this awareness will not naturally arise in people. Awareness is only possible through the dismantling of the false premises by which it is blocked. In this sense, teaching is indispensable. Socrates's midwifery contained within it this kind of paradox.

Socrates's method of question and answer is qualitatively different from what we usually mean by dialogue. Here two people with different opinions discuss and attempt to persuade each other. But Socrates only asks questions. The Socratic method is known through the works of Plato, but in fact it was of a different sort than represented there. The Platonic dialogue takes a fixed end point (telos) and proceeds toward it. This type of dialogue is in fact monologue, that is to say, internal reflection, and does not involve openness to the other. Dialogue with an actual other would not likely proceed so conveniently toward conclusion. For example, Diogenes Laërtius describes the Socratic method as follows: "Because, in discussing points that arose he often argued with great force, it often happened that he was beaten with fists, and pulled about by the hair, and laughed at and ridiculed by the multitude. But he bore all this with great equanimity. So that once, when he had been kicked and buffeted about, and had borne it all patiently, and someone expressed his surprise, he said, 'Suppose an ass had kicked me. Would you have had me file suit against him?'"[21]

The Socratic method involves destroying the other's false premises and chasing them into self-inconsistencies, and what follows after this cannot be predicted. Further, there is no guarantee that the resulting awareness will be of any duration. Hence, this process of dialogue was wrapped in peril. The wager of one's life was not limited to public affairs.

The significant characteristic of the Socratic dialogue, if we may call it so, is in fact in the asymmetry of the relation with the partner. This finds an analogy in the relation of analyst and analysand in the psychoanalytic method founded by Freud. This is called the talking cure, but differs from what we usually understand by conversation. It is rather closer to the delivery of the patient's awareness. Looking back from this point, one can imagine the extremes of transference and resistance brought about by the Socratic method. One could say these led ultimately to Socrates's death sentence.[22]

However, that Socrates saw virtue as a problem of the self is not to say that he introduced the level of the soul or notions of personal salvation. What Socrates ceaselessly kept in mind was the problem of the polis, that is to say the problem of politics, which is to say he discarded the dual world of public and private lives. But without the moment of each individual person's self-awareness, there is no way this can come about. Here a self that is neither public nor private is at stake.

Socrates left us no books. This indicates that the content of his thought resided in the one-on-one encounter with the other in dialogue. Plato, on the other hand, was an instructor at the Academy. He wrote his books in the format of the dialogue; however, this was a self-reflection, and not a dialogue with the other. This was his way of expressing his theories, in the form of the self-reflection of the logos (reason), and the Hegelian dialectic finds its prototype here.[23]

The negativity, uncertainty, and contingency that characterized the Socratic method are extinguished without a trace in Plato's works. Of course, this is not to imply that Plato did not wager himself as well. After experiencing the difficulty of making the philosopher a king, he thought instead to make the king a philosopher. Consequently, on the failure of his efforts to make Dionysius II of Syracuse into a philosopher, he was nearly sold into slavery. Certainly one can say here that Plato attempted dialogue with the other; however, that interlocutor was a king, not the people.

It was rather the minor Socratics who inherited the Socratic method. Diogenes, on hearing a group of boys gather round and say they were watching out that he didn't bite them, is said to have replied, "Don't worry, boys, a dog doesn't eat the green shoots." He likely learned this disposition at the foot of Socrates, who, enduring the violence of a man he enraged in debate, riposted, "If I was kicked by a donkey, would I name the animal in a suit at court?" Diogenes arguably inherited Socratic dialogue to a greater degree than Plato.

In contrast to Plato, Diogenes actually was sold as a slave. When asked what work he was capable of doing as a slave, he is said to have replied, "I can rule over people." At another time he lighted a candle in the daytime and walked around the square shouting, "Are there no humans here?" This verbal behavior constitutes a kind of Socratic method. Diogenes required a partner for this dialogue. Whether this caused people to look away in shame or brought their scorn he did not care. He is said, for example, to have been in the habit of masturbating in public. That is to say, he announced to the other that there is no need to hide physis.

PLATO AND PYTHAGORAS

Plato's first work records the testimony of Socrates in court regarding death as follows: "Let us reflect in another way, and we shall see that there is great reason to hope that death is a good; for one of two things—either death is a state of nothingness and utter unconsciousness, or, as men say, there is a change and migration of the soul from this world to another."[24] For Socrates, whichever the case may be, it will be to his profit. Socrates is concerned here neither to reject nor affirm the immortality of the soul. The meaning of his assertion is rather that there is a more important issue.[25] In the end, he says only this: "The hour of departure has arrived, and we go our ways—I to die, and you to live. Which is better God only knows."[26]

As discussed above, we can regard what is recorded in the *Apology*, in contrast to Plato's other dialogues, as based on fact. That is to say, what Socrates really thought about death was something close to this. However, beginning with *Crito* and *Phaedo*, which followed, Plato began to relate his own conceptions under the name Socrates. For example, in the *Phaedo*, the character Socrates states, as he is about to drink the poison, "For is not philosophy the study of death?" (232). That is to say, the task and concern of the philosopher are the liberation and separation of the soul from the flesh. However, this bears no resemblance to the thought of Socrates in the *Apology*. This line of thinking rather recalls that of the Pythagoreans.

Further, in addition to the idea of the immortality of the soul, Plato brings out in *Phaedo* the idea that things such as beauty, the good, size, and so forth exist in and of themselves. That is to say, in contrast to the objects of the senses, which are ceaselessly changing, the eternal and unchangeable exist as ideas. Sensory objects only participate in the idea (*eidos*). It was Aristotle who observed that this kind of thinking was inherited from Pythagoras. "Only the name 'participation' was new; for the Pythagoreans say that things exist by 'imitation' of numbers, and Plato says they exist by participation, changing [only] the name."[27]

Plato's theory of ideas, of course, differed from Pythagorean thought. Aristotle continues, "Further, besides sensible things and Forms [eidos] [Plato] says there are the objects of mathematics, which occupy an intermediate position, differing from sensible things in being eternal and unchangeable, from Forms in that there are many alike, while the Form itself is in each case unique."[28]

In Pythagoras's case, since his thought proceeds from number as its basis, sensible and suprasensible things are indissolubly linked. In Plato's case, however, the ideas (forms or eidos) exist in a realm separate from sensible things. In thinking of the combination and division of the two realms, sensible things and ideas, Pythagorean thought, where the two are inextricably linked from the start, provides no resources. Plato discerned the key for understanding the combination and division of the sensible and the ideal in the death of Socrates. Here he recognized the drama of the liberation of the idealistic object caught up in sensible things. In this way, the death of Socrates became the indispensable axis of Plato's philosophical system.[29]

Plato continued to bring the character Socrates onstage in his later works. It is obvious that this Socrates is a construct. Nevertheless, this has the effect of continually evoking the death of Socrates. In a word, Plato sought to legitimate his own struggle in the name of his teacher. But where was the conflict? It was a conflict with the opponents of his theory of ideas, specifically, with Ionian thought. In his later period he did not bother to conceal this intent. For example, in the *Sophist* Plato uses the analogy of the war raging between the Titans and the gods as an analogy for the struggle of (his) formalism versus (Ionian) materialism: "And that is the reason why [the materialists'] opponents cautiously defend themselves from above, out of an unseen world, mightily contending that true essence consists of certain intelligible and incorporeal ideas; the bodies of the materialists, which by them are maintained to be the very truth, they break up into little bits by their arguments, and affirm them to be, not essence, but generation and motion. Between the two armies, Theaetetus, there is always an endless conflict raging concerning these matters."[30]

In one of his final works, *Timaeus*, Plato essentially declares opposition to Ionian atheism and materialism. However, as discussed before, it is a mistake to see the Ionian natural philosophers as atheist. They believed that the One God exists, as nature. What they rejected were the personified gods. The Ionians discerned at the origin of things matter in motion. The gods are discovered when one posits a purpose based on one's retrospective observation of matter and its motion. Thus, the rejection of the personified gods by the natural philosophers is the rejection of a teleological worldview.

From this perspective, it is clear what Plato was trying to accomplish. This was of course not the naive restoration of the personified gods; it was rather the securing of a teleological worldview. This was why he had, at all costs, to refute the Ionian doctrine that matter moves of itself. In Plato's thought, there is an agent that originally brings about the motion of matter, which is God. The world does not arise through the motion of matter, but is a creation by God as the demiurge. Plato criticized Protagoras's notion that "man is the measure of all things," citing precisely God as the measure. However, Protagoras's attitude is not anthropocentric. Anthropocentrism rather resides in Plato, who posits a creator God based on his human perspective.

····················

THE PHILOSOPHER-KING

In Plato's *Menon*, the character of Socrates argues that coming to understand something is a process of recollection. It goes without saying that this is rooted in the Pythagorean idea of transmigration. More importantly, the idea of the philosopher-king proposed in *The Republic* also comes from Pythagoras. In *The Republic*, Socrates speaks as follows:

> And this was what we foresaw, and this was the reason why truth forced us to admit, not without fear and hesitation, that neither cities nor States nor individuals will ever attain perfection until the small class of philosophers whom we termed useless but not corrupt are providentially compelled, whether they will or not, to take care of the State, and until a like necessity be laid on the State to obey them; or

until kings, or if not kings, the sons of kings or princes, are divinely inspired with a true love of true philosophy.[31]

This kind of thinking cannot possibly come from Socrates. For Socrates, service to the state was strictly proscribed. That the idea of a philosopher-king is Plato's own is also clear from the The Seventh Letter, where Plato voices the identical opinion as his own. "And I was forced to say, when praising true philosophy that it is by this that men are enabled to see what justice in public and private life really is. Therefore, I said, there will be no cessation of evils for the sons of men, till either those who are pursuing a right and true philosophy receive sovereign power in the States, or those in power in the States by some dispensation of providence become true philosophers."[32]

The influence on Plato of the Pythagoreans was not only in abstract matters such as mathematics and transmigration. At the root was a more political problem. In order to confirm this, let us take a look at the itinerary Plato traveled to arrive at these opinions.

In The Seventh Letter, Plato describes his experience as a young man in great detail. "In my youth I went through the same experience as many other men. I fancied that if, early in life, I became my own master, I should at once embark on a political career. And I found myself confronted with certain occurrences in the public affairs of my own city." These "certain occurrences" were the despotism of the Thirty Tyrants engineered by his own aristocratic faction, among whom were many of Plato's relatives and friends. They sought to implicate Socrates in their deeds but were refused. Plato too chose not to participate in this order. The reign of the Thirty Tyrants shortly collapsed, and before long "once more, though with more hesitation, I began to be moved by the desire to take part in public and political affairs" (800).

Plato came to associate with Socrates toward the end of his life, but never considered living as he did. He never lost his aspiration to be involved in the affairs of the state. However, once the democratic faction brought capital charges against Socrates, Plato became suspect to both sides and found the road to politics closed off. In fact, foreseeing further retaliation by the democratic faction against the aristocrats after Socrates's death, he ended up fleeing Athens as well.

After the incident of Socrates's death (399 BCE), Plato commenced a period of wandering that lasted about ten years. It was during this time that he resolved to forgo politics and become a philosopher. "Finally, it became clear to me with regard to all existing communities, that they were one and all misgoverned. For their laws have got into a state that is almost incurable, except by some extraordinary reform with good luck to support it. And I was forced to say, when praising true philosophy that it is by this that men are enabled to see what justice in public and private life really is."[33] He then arrived at the statement of the philosopher-king quoted above. That he got the idea from the Pythagoreans is clear.

"With these thoughts in my mind," Plato writes, "I came to Italy and Sicily on my first visit." With the hope of putting his ideas about the philosopher-king into practice, Plato crossed over to Italy in 388 BCE, deepened his exchange with the Pythagoreans, and met their leader Archytas. Subsequently, Plato crossed to the island of Sicily and visited the tyrant of Syracuse, Dionysius I. But there he also met Dionysius's brother-in-law Dion, a beautiful youth who loved philosophy, and formed the hope that a government by philosopher-king might be realized in Syracuse.

However, Plato's political experience in Syracuse was disastrous. He was nearly sold into slavery after incurring the wrath of the tyrant Dionysius I and had to retreat hastily to Athens to escape. In Athens, then, he founded an academy resembling the school of the Pythagoreans. Plato subsequently returned to Syracuse two more times and suffered the same setbacks. He was, in a word, duped by the tyrants. However, it was not difficult to predict such an outcome, so it rather serves as evidence of how strong Plato's desire was to realize in practice the rule of the philosopher-king.

Looking at this turn of events, it is clear that Plato was drawn to the Pythagoreans for more than philosophical reasons. Democracy in Athens sent Socrates to his death. When Plato fled after this incident and commenced a period of wandering, he would have reflected on the nature of democracy. The doubt that presented itself was that, if the support of the majority is sufficient to legitimate a government, any degree of despotism can be allowed in their name. Here is how he expresses the problem:

> The excess of liberty, whether in States or individuals, seems only to pass into excess of slavery.
> Yes, the natural order.
> And so tyranny naturally arises out of democracy, and the most

aggravated form of tyranny and slavery out of the most extreme form of liberty?

As we might expect.[34]

What, then, is to be done? During the period he was mulling over this question, Plato came in contact with the school of the Pythagoreans. Here he found rule by philosophers. And, as discussed above, it was likely from this that he conceived the idea of the philosopher-king. However, this was not simply a matter of copying and influence. Given the political troubles he experienced in Athens, and the ten years of wandering after, Plato's understanding of Pythagoras's thought was honestly earned.

Let us summarize the earlier discussion of Pythagoras. On the island of Samos in Ionia, he had the painful experience of having his designs for political reform end in the establishment of tyranny. He left Ionia and commenced a long period of wandering, and after this founded on the south Italian coast a means of governance by philosopher. That Pythagoras founded an order was not due to the influence of the Orphic or Asian religions. It originates in his experience on Samos. The problem Pythagoras came face to face with first of all was the people. Left to their own devices, the freedom of the people ends in tyranny. The reason for this, according to Pythagoras, is that they are not truly free. They need to be released from the prison of their flesh. For this, an order is required. Second is the problem of the leader. Pythagoras's close friend Polycrates ended up a tyrant because of a problem residing within himself. The leader as well must become free from the yoke of the flesh. He must become a being that recognizes the true world that transcends the sensible world of appearance. That is to say, he must be a philosopher. Hence Pythagoras built an order ruled by a philosopher, through which he hoped to transform society.

ISONOMIA AND THE PHILOSOPHER-KING

Plato relates the idea of the philosopher king as if it were the idea of Socrates. However, the idea of the philosopher-king comes from Pythagoras and has little to do with Socrates. There was no way that Socrates, who declined public service all his life, would become king. Socrates rejected any thought that placed public affairs over private or spiritual matters over the physical. That is to say, he questioned both the Athenian and the Pythagorean versions of the dual world.

The Athenian dual world consists in the division between the public and private. Socrates sought to overcome that division as a private citizen. This is to effect transformation from below, the transformation of each individual. Next, to put it in terms of the Pythagorean dual world, Socrates never thought that he attained the world of truth. He felt himself to be ignorant in this sense. And he would attach himself like a gadfly to anyone who claimed to possess knowledge (truth), and engage him in the ceaseless interrogation of his method. What is called irony consists in this method. This is not a process that seeks to arrive at the world of truth. It aims at the idea of truth, or knowledge itself, as the premise on which the dual world of ignorance and knowledge is based.

Plato aimed at a condition where the soul ruled over the body. What Socrates aimed at, though, was the abolition of rule itself, that is to say, isonomia. Plato used the fact that Socrates was put to death by a democracy as a trump card. All through his career he championed Socrates and spoke in his name. However, this was a reverse implementation of Socrates's orientation. Socrates, whether unconsciously or not, recuperated the spirit of Ionian thought. Plato utilized this character as the greatest weapon in his own battle against this very Ionian thought.

In Plato, the thinking of Socrates is turned upside down. The philosopher is one who transcends the sensible world of semblance and grasps the truth. Further, this philosopher is active in public affairs, and through possession of political power realizes truth in the political world. "Until philosophers are kings, or the kings and princes of this world have the spirit and power of philosophy, and political greatness and wisdom meet in one, and those commoner natures who pursue either to the exclusion of the other are compelled to stand aside, cities will never have rest from their evils—no, nor the human race."[35]

In Plato, the ideal state will be realized when a philosopher like Socrates comes to rule. For him, "the truth is that the State in which the rulers are most reluctant to govern is always the best and most quietly governed."[36] However, this is not the sublation of rule. It is government by rulers who reject rule. In sum, the pursuit of a state of no-rule (isonomia) in Socrates becomes rule by the philosopher-king in Plato.

In the *Statesman*, Plato divides government into six possible forms. First is the division into three forms: rule by one, rule by the few, and rule

	RULE OF ONE	RULE BY THE FEW	RULE BY THE MANY
RULE OF LAW OBTAINS	Royalty	Aristocracy	Citizen-government
RULE WITHOUT LAW	Tyranny	Oligarchy	Democracy

TABLE 5.1 — Possible Forms of Government in Plato's *Statesman*

by the many. Within each of these forms then is distinguished a favorable form in which the rule of law is upheld, and a corrupted form in which law is scorned, yielding the following taxonomy (see table 5.1):

> This kind of classification is not original to Plato. According to Xenophon's notes, Socrates also conceived governing in this way. Plato's contribution is to attach a value to each form. In Plato's thinking, rule of one, when bound by good laws (royalty), is the best form. This is kingship. However, when the king holds the law in contempt, it becomes rather the worst possible form of rule, rule by tyranny. Rule by the few then, is intermediate between the two. Rule by the many or democracy, then is weak and inferior in every respect. However, compared to the other forms of rule in the case where the state holds the law in contempt, it is the least harmful.[37]

What is important here is that Plato conceived of a seventh possibility beyond these six. "If we divide each of these we shall have six, from which the true one may be distinguished as a seventh."[38] This is rule by the philosopher-king. "If they are all without restraints of law, democracy is the form in which to live is best; if they are well ordered, then this is the last which you should choose, as royalty, the first form, is the best, with the exception of the seventh, for that far excels them all, and is among States what God is among men."[39]

The form that occupies this seventh position does not exist anywhere in fact. That is to say, the state ruled by the philosopher-king is an idea. However, in a sense, Socrates too conceived this seventh position, nonexistent in fact. That would be isonomia. Socrates drew this out by contradiction (reductio ad absurdum) and did not demonstrate it in an active, positive manner. Plato, by contrast, presented this positively as an idea, located, so to speak, in heaven. We would call this the self-alienation of isonomia.

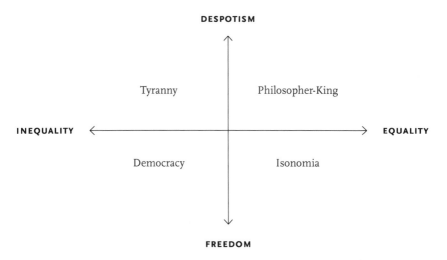

DESPOTISM

Tyranny   Philosopher-King

INEQUALITY ←——————————————→ EQUALITY

Democracy   Isonomia

FREEDOM

FIGURE 5.1 — Axis of Equality vs. Axis of Freedom

Let us take this opportunity to compare the ideas of Socrates and Plato on democracy. Socrates was critical of democracy. However, his reasoning differs from Plato. Subsequent to the reforms of Solon, the Athenian people came into contact with the Ionian spirit of isonomia (no-rule), but in reality settled on the degraded form of isonomia called democracy (rule of the many), a form constrained by the distinctions of public and private, and spiritual and manual labor. Socrates's aim was to dismantle the dual world of public and private existence that served as the premise of Athenian democracy. This meant nothing other than the restoration of isonomia. He carried out this task without consciously aiming to do so. That is to say, he operated under instructions from the daimon. As a result, he was not only held in contempt by the aristocratic faction, he was charged with a capital crime by the democrats.

Plato, on the other hand, held democracy itself responsible for Socrates's death. It is democracy itself that gives rise to tyranny and demagoguery. In order to evade this fate, what is required is not the opinions of the masses but an order ruled by philosophers. In this way, Plato turned toward a radical rejection of democracy. Here it would be worthwhile to specify the distinctions and indicate the structure relating isonomia, democracy, tyranny, and the philosopher-king (see figure 5.1).[40]

Plato took on as his life's work driving out the Ionian spirit that touched off Athenian democracy. The two crucial tasks were the rejection of the idea of the matter that moves of itself, which the Ionians arrived at through their critique of the gods, and the securing of the idea that the soul rules matter. This is clearly the construction of a theology. Moreover, Plato carried this project out from first to last under the name Socrates. As a result, from the time of Plato on, the origins of philosophy have been taken to reside in Socrates. And by extension, from the time of Nietzsche on, the critique of Plato has taken the form of an attack on Socrates, with the key to transcending Platonic philosophy taken to reside in the pre-Socratics. However, if one wants to properly consider the pre-Socratics, one must include Socrates in their number. Socrates was the last person to try to reinstitute Ionian thought and politics. In order to refute Platonic metaphysics and theology, it is precisely Socrates that is required.[41]

From *The Structure of World History* to
Isonomia and the Origins of Philosophy

My recent work, *The Structure of World History* (Duke University Press, 2014), is an attempt to look at the history of social formations from the perspective of modes of exchange. In this I follow Marx, who understood the history of social formations according to the economic base. Marx, however, examined the economic base in terms of modes of production. More specifically, this is to look at history in terms of ownership of the means of production. There are a number of difficulties, though, that attend this perspective. For example, it has difficulty dealing satisfactorily with premodern society and is unable to clarify its relation to the super-structure in terms of religion and nationalism, and so forth.

I felt it might be possible to deal with these difficulties by approaching the problem in terms not of modes of production, but modes of exchange. Of these I proposed the following typology:

MODE A   Reciprocity by gift and countergift
MODE B   Domination and protection
MODE C   Commodity exchange
MODE D   Mode that transcends A, B, and C

What we usually think of as exchange is commodity exchange, that is, mode C. However, in face-to-face communities such as the family and so forth, there is no exchange of this type, but rather a reciprocity consti-tuting gift giving and return, that is to say, mode of exchange A. Mode of exchange B, then, at first glance does not appear to have the exchange form. This is a type of relation where, in exchange for submission to the ruler, the ruled receive a sense of stability and security. The state is rooted in this form of exchange, which we call mode of exchange B. Mode of exchange C, then, while at first glance appearing to be an exchange based

B	A
Plunder and Redistribution	Reciprocity of the Gift
(Domination and Protection)	*(Gift and Countergift)*
C	**D**
Commodity Exchange	X
(Money and Commodities)	*(Yet to Be Realized)*

FIGURE APP.1 — Modes of Exchange

on freedom and equality, itself brings about a type of class relation different from the one that obtains in B, because of an asymmetry between the possessors of money and the possessors of goods and services.

Mode of exchange D, then, is the reintroduction of mode of exchange A on a higher level, after its dissolution by modes of exchange B and C. That is to say, D involves the recovery on a higher dimension of relations of reciprocity and mutual support, long after such actually existing societies were disintegrated by the rule of the state and the incursion of a money economy. What is important about D is, first of all, that unlike A, B, and C, it is realized on an imaginary level. Second, though we may characterize D as imaginary, that does not reduce it to a matter of personal desires and wishes; it is rather something brought into being in opposition to human will. This second point suggests to us the interesting fact that the path to mode of exchange D is first clearly shown in universal religions.

Any existing social formation is actually a composite of all four modes of exchange. However, they differ in terms of which mode of exchange can be said to be dominant. For example, in tribal societies prior to the development of the state, mode of exchange A is dominant. Elements of modes of exchange B and C do exist; however, they are suppressed and kept in check by the demands of A. Next, when the state is established over tribal societies, mode of exchange B becomes dominant; however, elements of modes of exchange A and C exist within it. For example, village life in agricultural communities persists under these conditions, and merchants and tradesmen may proliferate in the cities. However, these are controlled and regulated by the despotic or feudal state, that is to say,

B	A
B The State	**A** The Nation
C Capital	**D** X *(Yet to Be Realized)*

FIGURE APP.2 — The Structure of Capital = Nation = State

mode of exchange B. In a modern capitalist society, mode of exchange C is dominant. Modes of exchange A and B may persist, but only in an altered form, as for example when corvée labor and tribute are replaced in the modern state by conscription and taxes, or when the agricultural collective is altered into the imagined community of the nation. This is how the composite body of capital = nation = state is formed, and is the social formation under which we live today.

What is given above is an inquiry into the logic of the respective social formations. In fact, social formations do not exist in isolation, but rather in relation to other social formations. That is to say, they exist in a world system. Hence, a history of social formations must of necessity be considered a history of the world system. The history of the world system, just as with social formations, can be understood in terms of modes of exchange and divided in the same way into four stages.

First is the mini-world system (theorized by Christopher Chase-Dunn) given shape by mode of exchange A. Second is the system formed by mode of exchange B, or the world empire (Immanuel Wallerstein). Third is the system formed by mode of exchange C, or the world economy (also Wallerstein). The world economy existed in ancient Greece as well, but I will follow Immanuel Wallerstein in referring to the modern world economy in particular as the modern world system. Here, the governing social system takes the form of capital = nation = state. Finally, there is a new social formation that transcends each of these systems. This would be the world system given shape by mode of exchange D. When Kant referred to the world republic, he meant something like this.

B	A
World Empire	Mini-World System

C	D
World Economy	World Republic
(the Modern World System)	

FIGURE APP.3 — Stages of the World System

In addition to elucidating how transformations of the social formation, or world system, came to be, *The Structure of World History* investigates the question of how in the future a transition to a new world system might come about. A particularly important problem here is how the transition from a nomadic society to the first clan societies or tribal federations was effected. It has been generally accepted since Marcel Mauss that mode of exchange A (gift reciprocity) was the principle that governed archaic societies. However, it was not likely that anything like this principle existed in the earliest nomadic hunter-gatherer bands. Because their mobile lifestyle made the accumulation of goods impossible, things had to be pooled in common and distributed equally. This was a pure gift and not a return enforced by the reciprocal principle of gift exchange. As a result, the power of the group to enforce behavior in the individual was weak and conjugal relations fluid and impermanent. Consequently, each member of the group was free, at the same time they were equal.

By contrast, a clan society, which was based on the principle of reciprocity, was formed after nomadic people had permanently settled. Fixed settlements make possible the accumulation of wealth, but this is inevitably accompanied by disparities in wealth and power, and the separation of society into classes. Clan societies suppressed this danger through the obligations centering on the gift, and the return of the gift. This system did not come about through the positive will of the people involved. Rather, the pure gift-giving characteristic of the nomadic hunter-gatherer peoples reappears as the "return of the repressed" (in Freud) in compulsive form as the principle of reciprocity. In tribal society members are equal but are powerfully constrained by the community, and consequently cannot exist as free individuals.

The problem of the origins of tribal society is particularly significant for the following reason. Marx and Engels located a primitive communism in remote antiquity and presumed the communism of the future to lie in the recuperation of this primitive communism in advanced capitalism. The difficulty here is that they located primitive communism in Morgan's model in clan society. In my thinking, this needs to be located, not in clan society, but in the nomadic societies that preceded it.

Why then did they not attend to the difference between nomadic and clan societies? In a word, it is because they viewed the history of social formations from the perspective of modes of production. That is to say, in terms of mode of production, there is little difference between the two. However, if one looks from the perspective of modes of exchange, the difference between the two, that is to say the difference between the pure gift and the reciprocal exchange, or between the free individual and the individual bound by ties of reciprocity, is decisive.

The problem in setting clan society, with its constraints and forced relations, as the origin is that it becomes difficult to demonstrate the significance of recuperating this on a higher level. What follows rather is the kind of emphasis on collective possession of the means of production that gives rise to totalitarian society.

Mode of exchange A persists even when modes of exchange B and C are dominant. For example, regardless of how thorough the incursion of a money economy, A still persists in community and family. I defined mode of exchange D earlier as the recuperation of a heretofore suppressed mode of exchange A in the stage when modes B and C are dominant. However, D is not simply the restoration of A or the restoration of the older community. The recuperation of A on a higher level is not possible without its initial rejection.

Earlier I defined A as the compulsive return of the equality characteristic of nomadic society. Just as A appears in the form of compulsory obligations on the part of individuals, the negation of A must also take the form of a transcendence of individual will. In other words, it is not the case that D will emerge because individuals yearn for the return of A. D rather will appear as an imperative imposed on human beings by heaven or god. That is to say, in D the magic and reciprocal form of religion is negated, arriving as the universal form of religion.

Universal religion appeared in the time of the formation of the world empires, that is to say, during the time when clan society was being dissolved under the ascent of modes of exchange B and C, and the partition of society into classes was proceeding apace. This phenomenon arose in parallel in both West and East Asia from the sixth to the fifth centuries BCE.

Because universal religions seek to realize mode of exchange D in fact, they have the character of socialist movements. In fact, up until the nineteenth century, social movements arising in the various corners of the globe were almost always in the form of a universal religion. Subsequently the socialist movement repudiated any religious affiliation and became scientific. However, because that kind of socialism was ultimately only able to realize another society ruled by modes of exchange B and C, it lost its appeal. Nevertheless, as long as modes of exchange B and C remain dominant, the impulse to transcend them will never die. That is to say, in one form or another, mode D will be pursued. But does that necessarily have to take a religious form?

Universal religion is born of a critique of the religions affiliated with the state and community (modes of exchange B and A), that is to say, of the dominance of priests and officials. However, that critique is bound to be absorbed within a religious framework, that is to say, to revert to the dominance of a new caste of priests and officials. Another way of seeing this is to say religion ends up becoming the state itself. *The Structure of World History*, while giving due emphasis to the emergence of mode of exchange D on the one hand in the form of universal religions, poses the question of whether mode of exchange D might not take a nonreligious form. I then locate the first actual example of mode of exchange D, that is to say the return of mode of exchange A through the sublation of modes B and C, in the thought and politics of Ionia in ancient Greece. However, I was not able to develop this point sufficiently in *The Structure of World History*, and I take that opportunity now, in the current volume.

Timeline of the Ancient World

....

ALL DATES ARE BCE (BEFORE THE COMMON ERA).

CA. 1150   Settlement of the Attic peninsula after the fall of the Mycenaean civilization (ca. 1177 BCE).

CA. 1050   Migration of peoples from the Attic peninsula to the peripheries in Ionia and Sicily begins.

CA. 1000   David becomes king of Israel.

CA. 960   Solomon becomes king after David.

931   The unified state of Israel splits into the northern Israeli tribes and the kingdom of Judah to the south.

776   Olympic games in honor of Zeus opened.

CA. 750   City-states (poleis) proliferate all over the Greek territory. Colonies established in the Mediterranean and the Black Sea coast (Ionian colonies founded). Phonetic alphabet developed in the Greek peripheries.

CA. 730   The *Iliad* and *Odyssey* composed by Homer in Ionian dialect.

711   Assyria destroys the state of Israel.

CA. 700   Hesiod composes *Works and Days* and *Theogony*.

683   In Athens, the term of the archon, or magistrate, is limited to one year, signaling the stabilization of aristocratic rule.

CA. 660   Age of the lawgivers and tyrants in Greece (until ca. 500 BCE).

621   In Athens, harsh laws established under Draco (instability in aristocratic rule).

CA. 600   In Athens, bonded servitude of small and medium landholders proceeds apace.

597   Babylonian empire rules over Jerusalem (first Babylonian captivity). Tower of Babel, Hanging Gardens built in Babylon.

594   Reforms of Solon.

586   Babylon destroys Jerusalem, collapse of kingdom of Judah (second Babylonian captivity).

581   The city-states of Ionia are subjugated by the Lydian empire.

580	In Athens, the beginning of the tyranny of Peisistratus.
546	The city-states of Ionia undergo rule by the Persian successors to the Lydians. Persia conquers Babylon, unifying the region.
538	In Samos, tyranny of Polycrates.
508	Reforms of Cleisthenes (Athens).
499	Ionian revolt. Resistance breaks out across the Ionian city-states to Persian-backed tyrants installed since the subjugation. Athens sends a force to Ionia.
494	Miletus destroyed by the Persian army.
490	Outbreak of the Greco-Persian Wars. Greek troops defeat Persia at Marathon.
481	Thirty-one states of Greece form a league to oppose the Persian assault.
480	Second Persian invasion of Greece.
478	Delian League formed with Athens as head.
454	Athens transfers Delian army to its own control. Athenian empire.
449	End of the Greco-Persian Wars.
447	In Athens, building of the Parthenon.
443	Pericles establishes political leadership in Athens.
431	Outbreak of the Peloponnesian Wars.
430	Outbreak of plague in Athens, death of Pericles.
421	Athens, Sparta sign the Treaty of Nicias. Peace of Nicias ensues.
416	Athens invades the island of Melos, which had sided with Sparta in the Peloponnesian War, executes the male citizens, and enslaves the females.
413	War breaks out again between Sparta and Athens. City-states in the Athens League defect one by one. Sparta secures aid from Persia.
411	Coup by the oligarchy establishes rule by the Four Hundred in Athens.
404	Athens defeated by Sparta (end of the Peloponnesian Wars). The reign of the Thirty Tyrants established with Spartan backing.
403	In Athens, democratic governance restored. In Sicily, the reign of Dionysius.
399	Execution of Socrates in Athens.
388	Plato in itinerant life, crosses to Sicily.
387	Plato founds the Academy in Athens.
359	Philip II begins reign in Macedonia.
338	Macedonian army defeats Athens and Thebes in battle at Chaeronea.
336	Alexander III (the Great) succeeds Philip II as king of Macedonia.

Notes

INTRODUCTION

1   Cf. Weber: "The period of the older Israelitic prophecy at about the time of Elijah was an epoch of strong prophetic propaganda throughout the Near East and Greece . . . some of which reached into the sixth and even the fifth century. They were contemporary with Jewish, Persian, and Hindu prophetic movements, and probably also with the achievements of Chinese ethics in the pre-Confucian period." Max Weber, *The Sociology of Religion*, trans. Ephraim Fischoff (Boston: Beacon, 1964), 48–49.

2   Henri Bergson, *The Two Sources of Morality and Religion*, trans. Ashley Audra (New York: Doubleday, 1935), 267.

3   Weber, *The Sociology of Religion*, 25.

4   According to Koichi Namiki, it was on critical examination of their accumulated knowledge and ideas that they judged it appropriate to expound them as God's words. That is to say, it was their expressive style. "It is totally unconceivable that they did so in bad faith. Rather, they must have considered it to be discreet and effective, to efface the first person of the writer and direct their thoughts back to someone else other than themselves. If we don't grant this it is difficult to justify the extensive involvement of compilers and commentators in the prophetical books. However, after the editing of the book is completed, things started to appear differently." Koichi Namiki, *Kyûyaku-Seisho ni okeru Bunka to Ningen* [Culture and person in the Old Testament] (Tokyo: Kyobunkan, 1999), 28.

5   「無為自然」 or *wu wei zi ran*. This is a four-character phrase typical of Chinese rhetoric, with a number of possible connections between the first pair and second pair. In this case, wu wei or nonaction seems to lead to a "self-thusness" or naturalness. The second pair, zi ran or self-thusness, has come to idiomatically mean nature, but retains a logical sense in this phrase [translator's note].

6   This point explains why Laozi, regarded as the founder of Daoism, has repeatedly served as the philosophical source for anarchist social movements in Chinese history.

CHAPTER 1 · IONIAN SOCIETY AND THOUGHT

1   Hannah Arendt, *On Revolution* (New York: Penguin Classics, 1963), 20.

2   Aristotle, *Politics*, book 6, trans. Benjamin Jowett, in *Aristotle II* (Chicago: University of Chicago Press, 1952), 520. Note: All texts from the *Great Books* are available in a searchable database, at the Internet Classics Archive, http://classics.mit.edu.

3   Aristotle, *Politics*, 520.

4   Carl Schmitt, *Crisis of Parliamentary Democracy*, trans. Ellen Kennedy, Studies in Contemporary German Social Thought (Cambridge, MA: MIT Press, 1988), 9.

5   Euripides's tragedy *Ion* made current the view that the founder of Athens was Ion, that is, an Ionian, an ideology convenient to Athenian imperialism.

6   Translated into English from Hegel, *Tetsugakushi kôgi* [Lectures on the history of philosophy], trans. Hiroshi Hasegawa (Tokyo: Kawade Shobô, 1992), 147–49, with reference to http://www.marxists.org/reference/archive/hegel/works/hp/hpgreek .htm (no full translation available in English).

7   From Karl Marx, *The Ethnological Notebooks of Karl Marx*, ed. L. Krader (Assen, Netherlands: Van Gorcum, 1974), 213. Original excerpt reads: "Nur d. *unsettled conditions u. incessant warfare of the tribes* (Attic), from *their settlement in Attica bis zur zeit d. Solon* hatte die alte *gentile Organisation* so lang aufrecht erhalten können."

8   Lewis H. Morgan, *Ancient Society* (Chicago: Charles Kerr, 1877), 106. Found in http://archive.org/details/ancientsociety035004mbp.

9   Alain Testart, *Les chasseurs-cueilleurs ou l'origine des inégalités* [Of hunter-gatherers or on the origins of social inequality] (Paris: Société d'Ethnographie Université Paris X-Nanterre), 48–49. This follows Michael Bourdaghs's translation in Kōjin Karatani, *The Structure of World History*, 42, with reference to the Japanese edition, *Shin fubyôdô kigenron* (Tokyo: Hosei University Press), 54.

10 Herodotus, *The Histories*, book 2, v. 167, trans. George Rawlinson, in *Herodotus–Thucydides*, Great Books of the Western World (Chicago: University of Chicago Press, 1952), 85.

11 Herodotus, book 1, v. 170, 38.

12 Hegel, *Tetsugakushi kôgi*.

13 Arendt, *On Revolution*, 241.

14 Arendt, *On Revolution*, 208.

CHAPTER 2 · THE BACKGROUND OF IONIAN NATURAL PHILOSOPHY

1   Yôichi Hirokawa makes the following inference: "The tenth-century Byzantine encyclopedia and lexicon *Suda* records *On Nature* (Περι φυσεως), *Around the Earth* (Γης περιοδος), *On Fixed Bodies* (Περι των απλανων), *The Sphere* (Σφαιρα), and 'many other tomes' among Anaximander's works. . . . However, what is recorded in the *Suda* gives rather the impression that Anaximander's work was not limited to observation of the natural world, but ranged from history, to geography, to cultural history, and exhibited a wide scholarly range." Yôichi Hirokawa, *Socrates izen no tetsugakusha* (Tokyo: Kodansha, 1997), 56–57.

2   Translations are from Daniel W. Graham, ed. and trans., *The Texts of Early Greek Philosophy: The Complete Fragments and Selected Testimonies of the Major Presocratics* (Cambridge: Cambridge University Press, 2010). Fragment (F) and page number

are as follows: (1) f34, p. 633; (2) f86, p. 639; (3) f117, p. 647; (4) f2, p. 521; (5) f297, p. 681; (6) f259, p. 675.

3   Rosalind Thomas, *Herodotus in Context* (Cambridge: Cambridge University Press, 2000), 272–73.

4   Hippocrates, *On the Sacred Disease*, trans. Francis Adams, in *Hippocrates–Galen*, Great Books of the Western World, vol. 10 (Chicago: University of Chicago Press, 1952), 154–55. Translations are slightly amended for contemporary sense.

5   Hippocrates, *On the Sacred Disease*, 159. Greek φρενος is in English translation. Karatani further specifies nomos and physis.

6   "Alcmaeon," in *Stanford Encyclopedia of Philosophy*, revised June 10, 2013, http://plato.stanford.edu/entries/alcmaeon/.

7   From Alcidamas, "Messenian Speech," in *Classical Rhetoric and Rhetoricians*, ed. Michelle Ballif and Michael Moran (Westport, CT: Praeger, 2005), 15.

8   Aristotle, *Politics*, book 1, chap. 5, in *Aristotle II* (Chicago: University of Chicago Press, 1952), 448.

9   Thucydides writes, "The absence of romance in my history will, I fear, detract somewhat from its interest, but if it is judged worthy by those inquirers who desire an exact knowledge of the past as an aid to the understanding of the future, which in the course of human things must resemble if it does not reflect it, I shall be content. In fine I have written my work not as an essay with which to win the applause of the moment but as a possession for all time." Thucydides, *The History of the Peloponnesian War*, book 1, v. 22, trans. Richard Crawley, in *Herodotus–Thucydides* (Chicago: University of Chicago Press, 1952), 354. This is often regarded as a veiled criticism of Herodotus. Even if one doubts that, it is certainly the case that Thucydides's *History* carries a methodological will counter to that of Herodotus in the *Histories*.

10 Herodotus, *Histories*, book 2, chap. 158 (Chicago: University of Chicago Press, 1952), 83. Though earlier translators sometimes rendered this work *The History*, here we follow Rosalind Thomas and more recent scholars in using *Histories*.

11 Herodotus, *Histories*, book 2, chap. 50, 60.

12 Aristotle, *Politics*, book 7, chap. 7, 531–32.

13 Herodotus, *Histories*, book 3, 80, 107.

14 Herodotus, *Histories*, book 6, 43, 193.

15 Homer, *The Odyssey*, book 1, in *The Iliad of Homer/The Odyssey* (Chicago: University of Chicago Press, 1952), 183.

16 Hirono Seki, *Platon to shihonshugi* [Plato and capitalism] (Tokyo: Hokuto shuppan, 1996), 37.

17 Hesiod, *Works and Days*, in *Hesiod: Poems and Fragments*, trans. A. W. Mair (Oxford: Clarendon, 1908), vv. 80–107, p. 4. Available at http://files.libertyfund.org/files/1091/0606_Bk.pdf. Slightly amended.

18 Hesiod, *Works and Days*, vv. 167–93, p. 7.

19 Hesiod, *Works and Days*, vv. 248–76, p. 10.

20 Hesiod, *Works and Days*, vv. 306–35, p. 12.

21 George Thomson, *The First Philosophers: Studies in Ancient Greek Society* (London: Lawrence and Wishart, 1955), 196.

22 Gilbert Murray finds in the emergence of the gods of Olympus a "reformation," which according to my understanding signifies a leap from tribal religions. However, the "transformation" I refer to here is peculiar to Ionia, and disappears with Ionia's fall. Murray does give some attention to the case of Ionia. "And lastly, we must remember that Ionia was, before the rise of Athens, not only the most imaginative and intellectual part of Greece, but by far the most advanced in knowledge and culture. The Homeric religion is a step in the self-realization of Greece, and such self-realization naturally took its rise in Ionia." Gilbert Murray, *Five Stages of Greek Religion* (New York: Columbia University Press, 1925), 81–82. Murray pays no attention whatsoever, though, to the historical particularity of Ionia.

23 Aristotle, *Metaphysics*, book 1, chap. 1, in *Aristotle I* (Chicago: University of Chicago Press, 1952), 500.

24 Hesiod, *Works and Days*, vv. 220–47, p. 9, slightly amended.

CHAPTER 3 · THE ESSENTIAL POINTS OF IONIAN NATURAL PHILOSOPHY

1 From "Anaximander," in *The Texts of Early Greek Philosophy: The Complete Fragments and Selected Testimonies of the Major Presocratics*, ed. and trans. Daniel W. Graham (Cambridge: Cambridge University Press, 2010), F1, p. 51, slightly amended.

2 Aristotle, *Metaphysics*, book 1, chap. 3, 501–2.

3 Aristotle, *De anima*, book 1, chap. 5, trans. J. A. Smith, in *Aristotle I* (Chicago: University of Chicago Press, 1952), 641.

4 According to Simplicius in the *Physics*, "[Like Anaximander], Anaximenes himself says, that the underlying nature is single and boundless, but not indeterminate as he says, but determinate, calling it air. It differs in essence in accordance with its rarity or density. When it is thinned it becomes fire, while when it is condensed it becomes wind, then cloud, when still more condensed, water, then earth, then stones. Everything else comes from these. And he too makes motion everlasting, as a result of which change occurs." "Anaximenes," in *The Texts of Early Greek Philosophy*, 75, slightly amended.

5 The idea that the world is generated from the single substance called the boundless in fact has an affinity with idealism such as Fichte's or dialectics such as Hajime Tanabe's "absolute negativity."

6 Aristotle himself did not use the word *metaphysics* or describe his work that way. He called the field that inquires into the basis of natural science (physics) "first philosophy." The word *metaphysics* was applied to a number of assembled texts by editors in the first century CE. This inquiry that follows the *Physics* was called

literally meta-physics (after, or beyond, the physics). It was afterward that "first philosophy" was used to indicate this assembly of texts.

7   Translation is from the German, in Ernst Bloch, *Vorlesungen zur Philosophie der Renaissance* (Frankfurt: Suhrkamp, 1972), 116. Karatani refers to the Japanese translation in Bloch, 『ルネサンスの哲学』 [Philosophy of the Renaissance], trans. Chika Yoshikawa (Tokyo: Hakusuisha, 2005), 158.

8   Bloch, *Vorlesungen zur Philosophie der Renaissance*, 39.

9   Spinoza, letter 56 (60), to Hugo Boxel, 1674, translated from the Japanese in *Tetsugaku no kigen*, p. 101.

10 "Xenophanes," in *The Texts of Early Greek Philosophy*, 109–11, FF19–21.

11 "Xenophanes," III, F23.

12 Aristotle, *Metaphysics*, book 11, chap. 7, 592; book 6, chap. 1, 547.

13 Benjamin Farrington, *Greek Science: Its Meaning for Us* (New York: Penguin, 1949), 38.

14 Farrington, *Greek Science*, 38–39.

15 Aristotle, *Physics*, book 2, chap. 8, 276.

16 Chikatsugu Iwasaki. 『ギリシア•ポリス社会の哲学』 [The philosophy of polis society in Greece] (Tokyo: Miraisha, 1994), 188.

17 Diodorus Siculus, *The Library of History*, trans. C. H. Oldfather, Loeb Classical Library (Cambridge, MA: Harvard University Press, 1967), book 1, chap. 8. Reproduced in http://penelope.uchicago.edu/Thayer/E/Roman/Texts/Diodorus_Siculus/. Karatani uses the quotation in Benjamin Farrington, *Greek Science* (Chester Springs, PA: Dufour Editions, 1981).

18 Ionian evolutionary theory disappeared with the fall of the Roman Empire and the ascendancy of the Catholic Church; however, we should bear in mind it was incorporated into Islamic thought. In particular, the ninth-century scholar Al-Jahiz (781–868) describes the living organism's chance for existence and the influence of environment as a "struggle for existence" in his *Book of Animals*. Ibn Miskawayh (932–1030) describes the succession of life forms as a kind of evolution, wherein steam assumes the form of water, and in time there follows mineral life, then plant life, animals, primates, and then humans. Ibn Al-Haytham (965–1040), Ibn Haldun (1332–1406), and others engaged in debates on evolutionary thought. Their works were translated into Latin, and exercised a direct influence on Renaissance thought.

19 The biologist Motô Kimura introduced a supposedly anti-Darwinian neutral theory of molecular evolution. According to this theory, most of the variations are neither beneficial nor deleterious but neutral for the organism's survival. However, Darwin did not posit directionality or teleology in variation, as is generally believed. This misunderstanding stems from Darwin's borrowing of the term "survival of the fittest" from Herbert Spencer. Regarding the survivors in the natural world as the fittest is only in hindsight, which reinstates once-negated teleology.

1 George Thomson, *The First Philosophers: Studies in Ancient Greek Society* (London: Lawrence and Wishart, 1955), 256.

2 Thomson, *The First Philosophers*, 254.

3 Polycrates was asked to visit a person an oracle prophesied would assassinate him, duly set out, and was killed in short order. In psychology, desire for self-punishment is called a Polycrates complex.

4 Nietzsche, *The Will to Power*, translated from the Japanese, with reference to the translation by Lucovici (London: Allen Unwin, 1909), book III, note 586.

5 Karl Marx, *The German Ideology*, in *The Marx-Engels Reader*, ed. Robert Tucker (New York: W. W. Norton, 1978), 158–59.

6 F. M. Cornford, *Principium Sapientiae: The Origins of Greek Philosophical Thought* (New York: Harper and Brothers, 1952).

7 The trade of the Pythagoreans was casting metal coins. However, it is not likely that they thought, as the alchemists would later, that some power lay in the metals themselves. Where does the power of money lie? Marx deals with this problem in *Capital*. There he discerned that the power of money does not lie in the material properties of gold and silver, but in the social relations formed through commodity exchange. Here all commodities express their own worth in relation to a single value form, in other words, money form. This would appear to assign a special power to the single commodity that occupies that position. However, the magical spell of currency, like that of music, lies in the relation itself.

8 Anaximander held the position that the stars were orbs of fire. Anaxagoras held, after Pythagoras, that the sun was a red hot stone and the moon composed of earth, and was driven out of Athens for this blasphemy toward the heavenly bodies. By contrast, Pythagoras grasped the heavenly bodies solely in their aspect as relation, which is not to say that he placed the "heavenly bodies" in a theological perspective. It is Aristotle who reported that the Pythagoreans maintained a species of heliocentric theory. "As to [the earth's] position, there is some difference of opinion. Most . . . say it lies at the centre. But the Italian philosophers known as Pythagoreans take the contrary view. At the centre, they say, is fire, and the earth is one of the stars, creating night and day by its circular motion about the centre. They further construct another earth in opposition to ours, to which they give the name counter-earth." Aristotle, *On the Heavens*, chapter 13, trans. J. L. Stocks, in *Aristotle I* (Chicago: University of Chicago Press, 1952), 384. This fire at the center was not the sun, but something not visible to the eye, the sun being one of the planets in motion about this center. The planets numbered nine, including the sun and moon, and if to this is added the sphere of the fixed stars, there were a total of ten heavenly bodies in motion around the fire fixed at the center. This account by the Pythagoreans then influenced the heliocentric theory of the Early Hellenic astronomer and mathematician Aristarchus. By some accounts Copernicus knew of the Pythagorean theories through Plutarch's *Of Those Sentiments*

Concerning Nature with Which the Philosophers Were Delighted, and began entertaining the possibility of a heliocentric theory as a result.

9 Karl Popper, *The Open Society and Its Enemies* (Princeton, NJ: Princeton University Press, 1963), 12.

10 From "Heraclitus," in *The Texts of Early Greek Philosophy: The Complete Fragments and Selected Testimonies of the Major Presocratics*, ed. and trans. Daniel W. Graham (Cambridge: Cambridge University Press, 2010), F1, 51, slightly amended.

11 Trans. note: Karatani uses the system for numbering fragments in Hermann Diels, *Die Fragmente der Vorsokratiker*, ed. Walther Kranz (Berlin: Weidmann, 1951–52). Fragments from Heraclitus will give the sequence number used in Graham, *The Texts of Early Greek Philosophy* (above), followed by Diels in this format: (143, B121).

12 Hideya Yamakawa. *Kodai girishia no shisô* [Ancient Greek thought] (Tokyo: Kodansha gakujutsu bunko), 112.

13 "Anaximander," in *The Texts of Early Greek Philosophy*, 50–51.

14 "Xenophanes," in *The Texts of Early Greek Philosophy*, 110–11.

15 Aristotle, *Metaphysics*, 504.

16 For example, the classical economists (Smith and Ricardo) thought as follows. In any commodity there is a shared essence that consists of the value of the labor added in production. What expresses this value is money. Exchange was unimportant for them. However, when people exchange different commodities, this is not because they have the same value; it is because of a mutual desire for their use value. As a result, one can discover a common essence in different commodities. Further, through exchange, one commodity in particular is elevated to the level of currency (general equivalence). As a result, this one commodity (gold or silver) becomes money. Marx proposed this kind of idea in *Capital*. Marx is often thought to have inherited the labor theory of value from the classical economists, but he rather reintroduced the possibilities of exchange erased in the classical critique of mercantilism or merchant capitalism.

17 "Parmenides," in *The Texts of Early Greek Philosophy*, 15, F6.

18 Translated to English from the Japanese, Hegel, *Tetsugakushi kôgi* [Lectures on the history of philosophy], trans. Hiroshi Hasegawa (Tokyo: Kawade Shobô, 1992), 268–69, with reference to the unattributed English translation available at http://www.marxists.org/reference/archive/hegel/works/hp/hpgreek.htm.

19 Hegel, *Tetsugakushi kôgi*, 265.

20 Diogenes Laërtius, *Life of Zeno the Eleatic*, book 9, chap. 5, in *Lives and Opinions of the Eminent Philosophers*.

21 Aristotle, *Metaphysics*, 504–5.

22 Yamakawa, *Kodai girishia no shisô*, 178.

23 "Parmenides," 214–17, fragment B8.

24 "Parmenides," fragments F3 and F4, 212–13. This is supplemented by the translation at Albino Nolletti, "The 'Vision' and Reasoning of Parmenides," 2013, http://www.parmenides-of-elea.net/ (8, 24–26).

25 Kant, letter to M. Hertz, May 11, 1781, in *Immanuel Kant: Philosophical Correspondence 1759–1799*, ed. Arnold Zweig (Chicago: University of Chicago Press, 1967).

26 "Parmenides," 218–19.

27 "Empedocles," in *The Texts of Early Greek Philosophy*, 344–47.

28 "Empedocles," 348–49.

29 "Anaxagoras," in *The Texts of Early Greek Philosophy*, 284–85.

30 Cf. Anaxagoras, "Together were all things, boundless both in quantity and in smallness" (280–81).

31 Aëtius (pseudo-Plutarch), book 1, chap. 17, verse 3 in *Opinions of the Philosophers*.

32 "Empedocles," 338–39.

33 "Empedocles," 332–33.

34 "Democritus' Ethical Fragments," in *The Texts of Early Greek Philosophy*, 680–81.

CHAPTER 5 · SOCRATES AND EMPIRE

1 Arendt distinguishes between empire and imperialism as follows: "Conquest as well as empire-building had fallen into disrepute for very good reasons. They had been carried out successfully only by governments which, like the Roman Republic, were based primarily on law, so that conquest could be followed by integration of the most heterogeneous peoples by imposing upon them a common law. The nation-state, however, based upon a homogeneous population's active consent to its government (Renan's 'le plébiscite de tous les jours'), lacked such a unifying principle and would, in the case of conquest, have to assimilate rather than to integrate, to enforce consent rather than justice, that is, to degenerate into tyranny." Hannah Arendt, *The Origins of Totalitarianism* (New York: Houghton Mifflin, 1968), chapter 5, part 1: Political Emancipation of the Bourgeoisie.

2 Thucydides's *History* as well as Aristophanes's *Lysistrata* both illustrate the role of the aristocratic faction in arguing for peace between the poleis.

3 Pericles enacted the laws that denied Athenian citizenship to persons of foreign origin. However, after he lost his own son to war, he attempted to give special citizenship to the son of his union with the courtesan Aspasia, a native of Miletus, at some risk to his own standing.

4 It was not only male immigrants from Ionia who were active on the Athenian intellectual scene. For example, Aspasia, the Milesian courtesan Pericles took as his concubine, was said to have written the drafts of his speeches. Socrates is also said to have learned rhetoric from this woman. Aspasia was undoubtedly an exceptional case; however, when we consider that Athenian women were virtually completely excluded from the public space, her genius was not simply an individual matter, but a product of the social environment of Ionia.

5   Plato, *Protagoras*, trans. Benjamin Jowett, in *Plato*, Great Books of the Western World (Chicago: University of Chicago Press, 1952), 52.

6   Diogenes Laërtius, *Lives and Opinions of the Eminent Philosophers*, book 2, *Life of Socrates*, chap. 19.

7   Callicles's intervention begins in *Gorgias*, in *Plato*, 271–73.

8   Plato, *The Republic*, in *Plato*, book 6, 377.

9   Diogenes Laërtius, *Lives and Opinions of the Eminent Philosophers*, book 2, chap. 8.

10   Plato, *Apology*, in *Plato*, 207.

11   Plato, *Apology*, 209.

12   Marx writes, "Human emancipation will only be complete when the real, individual man has absorbed into himself the abstract citizen; when as an individual man, in his everyday life, in his work, and in his relationships, he has become a *species-being*; and when he has recognized and organized his own powers (*forces propres*) as *social* powers so that he no longer separates this social power from himself as *political* power." From Karl Marx, *On the Jewish Question*, in *The Marx-Engels Reader*, ed. Robert C. Tucker (New York: W. W. Norton, 1978), 46.

13   Xenophon, *Memorabilia*, ed. D. C. Marchant, Tufts University Perseus Digital Library, book 3, chap. 4.

14   Xenophon, *Memorabilia*, book 3, chap. 6.

15   Xenophon, *Memorabilia*, book 2, chap. 8.

16   Within the sphere of human activity, Hannah Arendt places public action over labor. And she explicates this as a standard of Athenian society. If we take this view, Socrates's activities would be deemed meaningless. Despite Arendt's criticism of democracy, which she differentiated from isonomia, in the end she reveals support of Athenian democracy.

17   Plato, *Apology*, 207.

18   Aristophanes, *The Clouds*, Internet Classics Archive, http://classics.mit.edu/Aristophanes/clouds.html. Cf. Aristophanes, *The Clouds*, trans. Benjamin B. Rogers, Great Books of the Western World (Chicago: University of Chicago Press, 1952), 493, amended.

19   Adapted with minimal adjustment from Hegel, "Socrates," in *Hegel's Lectures on the Philosophy of History*, http://www.marxists.org/reference/archive/hegel/works/hp/hpgreek.htm. No complete published translation available in English.

20   Plato, *Apology*, 207.

21   Adapted from Diogenes Laërtius, *Lives and Opinions of the Eminent Philosophers*, book 2, chap. 7.

22   Freud, in the early stages of the psychoanalytic movement, seeing the failure of treatment due to the romantic state brought about by transference between analyst and analysand, sought to instill a consciousness of psychoanalytic treatment as a business transaction by collecting money from the patient. In this light, Socrates

was regarded as corrupting the youth of Athens even more than the Sophists, precisely because he did not accept money for his services.

23 The dialectic manifests itself in Plato in the following way: "This is that strain which is of the intellect only, but which the faculty of sight will nevertheless be found to imitate; for sight, as you may remember, was imagined by us after a while to behold the real animals and stars, and last of all the sun himself. And so with dialectic; when a person starts on the discovery of the absolute by the light of reason only, and without any assistance of sense, and perseveres until by pure intelligence he arrives at the perception of the absolute good, he at last finds himself at the end of the intellectual world, as in the case of sight at the end of the visible. . . . Then dialectic, and dialectic alone, goes directly to the first principle and is the only science which does away with hypotheses in order to make her ground secure; the eye of the soul, which is literally buried in an outlandish slough, is by her gentle aid lifted upwards; and she uses as handmaids and helpers in the work of conversion, the sciences which we have been discussing." Plato, *The Republic*, book 7, 397–98.

24 Plato, *Apology*, 211.

25 Socrates's meditation on death recalls the words of Confucius from the *Analects*: "not yet even knowing life, how can you seek to know death?" (*Analects*, book 2, part 11) and, "Of portents, wonders, disorder, and heavenly beings, the Master passed over in silence." (*Analects*, Book 2, Part 7, translated from classical Japanese citation). Confucius does not deny here the existence of the gods or the afterlife. He simply says that there is something more important.

26 Plato, *Apology*, 212.

27 Aristotle, *Metaphysics*, book 1, chap. 6, trans. Benjamin Jowett, in *Aristotle I and II*, Great Books of the Western World (Chicago: University of Chicago Press, 1952), 505.

28 Aristotle, *Metaphysics*.

29 Just as Plato used the death of Socrates as the axis of his metaphysics, Paul discovered in the death of Christ the key for the connection of God and man. Just as Plato created a theology based on Socrates's death, so Paul created Christian theology based on Jesus's death.

30 Plato, *Sophist*, trans. Benjamin Jowett, in *Plato*, 567.

31 Plato, *The Republic*, book 6, 381.

32 Plato, *The Seventh Letter*, trans. J. Harward, in *Plato*, 801.

33 Plato, *The Seventh Letter*, 801.

34 Plato, *The Republic*, book 8, 412–13.

35 Plato, *The Republic*, book 5, 369.

36 Plato, *The Republic*, book 7, 391.

37 This discussion is found in Plato, *Statesman*, in *Plato*, 603ff. Aristotle's *Politics* reprises the classification, though Aristotle sharply criticizes the arguments of *The Republic*.

38 Plato, *Statesman*, 603.

39   Plato, *Statesman*, 604.

40   Karl Popper, in *The Open Society and Its Enemies,* uses the concept of isonomia.
      According to Popper, isonomia consists in the following three principles: (1) birth,
      lineage, wealth, and other natural privileges are not recognized; (2) it is individu-
      alist; and (3) the duty and goal of the state is to secure the freedom of the citizens.
      By contrast, Plato's state is presented as a term-for-term opposition: (1) natural
      privilege is recognized; (2) it is a kind of totalitarianism; and (3) the duty and goal
      of the individual is to support and strengthen the state. Consequently, Plato is the
      enemy of the open society. However, what Popper presents as isonomia is not
      worthy of the name. It is similar to Athenian democracy, or more to American
      liberal democracy. Here people are equal under the law but unequal economically.
      Consequently, democracy (rule by the many) consists in the majority taking power
      and dissipating inequality by redistribution. By contrast, isonomia indicates a sys-
      tem in which all are not merely equal under the law, but conditions are such that
      economic divisions also do not arise. This is the isonomia that existed in Ionia but
      not in Athens. What existed in Athens was democracy, which in times of crisis
      shifted naturally to tyranny or rule by demagoguery.
            The next important point is to draw the similarities and differences between
      tyranny and the rule of the philosopher-king. In the twentieth century, fascism
      would be a case where tyranny and demagoguery arose from democracy. By con-
      trast, what corresponds to Plato's philosopher-king would be Bolshevism (or Le-
      ninism). This was a rule based on reason. Popper ranges liberal democracy over
      against these two. Liberal democracy, though, is not a true open society. As with
      Athenian democracy, contemporary liberal democracy carries within it a num-
      ber of contradictions. The idea of the philosopher-king met its death along with
      the fall of the Soviet Union. The Hegelian Francis Fukuyama declared at that
      point the end of history with the victory of liberal democracy. However, while the
      philosopher-king is probably no longer viable as a principle for governing, lib-
      eral democracy has been only incompletely instituted as well. What is completely
      erased in these debates, though, is the idea of isonomia.

41   The critique of metaphysics as it developed after Plato is typically, as with Nietz-
      sche, carried out by praising the pre-Socratics. Derrida is an exception within this
      strain. In Derrida's deconstruction, a proposition is first accepted, then by drawing
      out from those premises precisely the negation of that proposition, one is driven
      into an indeterminacy, and the proposition is driven into self-destruction. How-
      ever, this is the same as Socrates's method. Derrida sought to carry out his critique
      of Platonic metaphysics through the reintroduction, not of the pre-Socratics, but
      of Socrates himself. However, he himself did not make this clear. Another figure
      in the critique of metaphysics, Michel Foucault, did not speak of the pre-Socratics.
      Rather, Foucault, in the final lectures before his death called "The Courage of
      Truth," attempted a positive reappraisal of the philosophy Socrates had opened
      up. Here he saw Socrates as a person in possession of parrhesia, or speaking the
      truth. Of course, the aspect of Socrates that is the object of reevaluation here is
      not the metaphysical aspect that leads to Plato, but rather the practical aspect that
      leads to Diogenes. In that sense, it could be said that Foucault found the key to the
      struggle against Platonic metaphysics in Socrates.

Bibliography

....

Presocratic Philosophers (Thales, Anaximander, Anaximenes, Xenophanes, Heraclitus, Parmenides, Anaxagoras, Empedocles; Atomists: Leucippus and Democritus) can be found in Daniel W. Graham, ed. and trans., *The Texts of Early Greek Philosophy: The Complete Fragments and Selected Testimonies of the Major Presocratics*. 2 vols. Cambridge: Cambridge University Press, 2010.

Arendt, Hannah. *On Revolution*. New York: Penguin Classics, 1963.

———. *The Origins of Totalitarianism*. New York: Houghton Mifflin, 1968.

Aristophanes. *The Clouds*. Internet Classics Archive. http://classics.mit.edu/Aristophanes/clouds.html.

Aristotle. *De anima*. Translated by J. A. Smith. In *Aristotle I*. Great Books of the Western World, vol. 8. Chicago: University of Chicago Press, 1952.

———. *Metaphysics*. Translated by W. D. Ross. In *Aristotle I*. Great Books of the Western World, vol. 8. Chicago: University of Chicago Press, 1952.

———. *On the Heavens*. Translated by J. L. Stocks. In *Aristotle I*. Great Books of the Western World, vol. 8. Chicago: University of Chicago Press, 1952.

———. *Physics*. Translated by R. P. Hardie and R. K. Gaye. In *Aristotle I*. Great Books of the Western World, vol. 8. Chicago: University of Chicago Press, 1952.

———. *Politics*. Translated by Benjamin Jowett. In *Aristotle II*. Great Books of the Western World, vol. 9. Chicago: University of Chicago Press, 1952.

Aristotle I and II. Great Books of the Western World, vols. 8 and 9. Chicago: University of Chicago Press, 1952.

Ballif, Michelle, and Michael Moran, eds. *Classical Rhetoric and Rhetoricians*. Westport, CT: Praeger, 2005.

Bergson, Henri. *The Two Sources of Morality and Religion*. Translated by Ashley Audra. New York: Doubleday, 1935.

Bloch, Ernst. *Runesansu no tetsugaku* [Vorlesungen zur Philosophie der Renaissance]. Translated by Yoshikawa, Chika. Tokyo: Hakusuisha, 2005.

Cornford, F. M. *Principium Sapientiae: The Origins of Greek Philosophical Thought*. New York: Harper and Row, 1952.

Diels, Hermann. *Die Fragmente der Vorsokratiker*, 3 vols. Edited by Walther Kranz. Berlin: Weidmann, 1951–52.

Diodorus Siculus. *The Library of History*. Translated by C. H. Oldfather. Loeb
    Classical Library. Cambridge, MA: Harvard University Press, 1967. http://
    penelope.uchicago.edu/Thayer/E/Roman/Texts/Diodorus_Siculus/.

Diogenes Laërtius. *Lives and Opinions of the Eminent Philosophers*. Translated by
    C. D. Yonge. http://classicpersuasion.org/pw/diogenes/index.htm.

Farrington, Benjamin. *Greek Science*. New York, Penguin, 1961.

———. *Greek Science: Its Meaning for Us*. New York: Penguin, 1949.

Hahn, Robert. *Archaeology and the Origins of Philosophy*. Albany: State University
    of New York Press, 2011.

Hegel, G. F. W. *Tetsugakushi kôgi* [Lectures on the history of philosophy]. Trans-
    lated by Hiroshi Hasegawa. Tokyo: Kawade Shobô, 1992. With reference
    to partial translation at http://www.marxists.org/reference/archive/hegel
    /works/hp/hpgreek.htm.

Herodotus. *The Histories*. Translated by George Rawlinson. In *Herodotus–Thu-
    cydides*. Great Books of the Western World. Chicago: University of Chicago
    Press, 1952.

Hesiod. *Works and Days*. In *Hesiod: Poems and Fragments*. Translated by A. W.
    Mair. Oxford: Clarendon, 1908. http://files.libertyfund.org/files/1091
    /0606_Bk.pdf.

Hippocrates. *On the Sacred Disease*. Translated by Francis Adams. In *Hippo-
    crates–Galen*. Great Books of the Western World, vol. 10. Chicago: Univer-
    sity of Chicago Press, 1952.

Hirokawa, Yôichi. *Socrates izen no tetsugakusha* [Philosophers before Socrates].
    Tokyo: Kodansha, 1997.

Homer. *The Odyssey*, book 1. In *The Iliad of Homer/The Odyssey*. Great Books of
    the Western World. Chicago: University of Chicago Press, 1952.

Iwasaki, Chikatsugu. *Girishia porisu shakai no tetsugaku* [Philosophy of the Greek
    polis]. Tokyo: Miraisha, 1995.

Kant, Immanuel. *Immanuel Kant: Philosophical Correspondence 1759–1799*. Edited
    by Arnold Zweig. Chicago: University of Chicago Press, 1967.

Karatani, Kôjin. *The Structure of World History*. Translated by Michael Bourd-
    aghs. Durham, NC: Duke University Press, 2014.

Mansfeld, Jaap. *The Body Politic: Aëtius on Alcmaeon on Isonomia and Monarchia*.
    Cambridge: Cambridge University Press, 2013.

Marx, Karl. *The Ethnological Notebooks of Karl Marx*. Edited by L. Krader. Assen,
    Netherlands: Van Gorcum, 1974.

———. *The German Ideology*. In *The Marx-Engels Reader*. Edited by Robert
    Tucker. New York: W. W. Norton, 1978.

Morgan, Lewis H. *Ancient Society*. Chicago: Charles Kerr, 1877. http://archive
    .org/details/ancientsociety035004mbp.

Murray, Gilbert. *Five Stages of Greek Religion*. New York: Columbia University Press, 1925.

Namiki, Kôichi. *Kyûyaku Seisho ni okeru bunka to ningen* [Culture and person in the Old Testament]. Tokyo: Kyobunkan, 1999.

Nietzsche, Friedrich. *Will to Power*. Translated by Anthony M. Ludovici. London: Allen and Unwin, 1909.

Plato. *Apology*. Translated by Benjamin Jowett. In *Plato*. Great Books of the Western World. Chicago: University of Chicago Press, 1952.

———. *Gorgias*. Translated by Benjamin Jowett. In *Plato*. Great Books of the Western World. Chicago: University of Chicago Press, 1952.

———. *Protagoras*. Translated by Benjamin Jowett. In *Plato*. Great Books of the Western World. Chicago: University of Chicago Press, 1952.

———. *The Republic*. Translated by Benjamin Jowett. In *Plato*. Great Books of the Western World. Chicago: University of Chicago Press, 1952.

———. *The Seventh Letter*. Translated by J. Harward. In *Plato*. Great Books of the Western World. Chicago: University of Chicago Press, 1952.

———. *Sophist*. Translated by Benjamin Jowett. In *Plato*. Great Books of the Western World. Chicago: University of Chicago Press, 1952.

———. *Statesman*. Translated by Benjamin Jowett. In *Plato*. Great Books of the Western World. Chicago: University of Chicago Press, 1952.

Popper, Karl. *The Open Society and Its Enemies*. Princeton, NJ: Princeton University Press, 1963.

Schmitt, Carl. *Crisis of Parliamentary Democracy*. Translated by Ellen Kennedy. Studies in Contemporary German Social Thought. Cambridge, MA: MIT Press, 1988.

Seki, Hirono. *Platon to shihonshugi* [Plato and capitalism]. Tokyo: Hokuto shuppan, 1996.

Testart, Alain. *Les chasseurs-cueilleurs ou l'origine des inégalités* [Of hunter-gatherers or on the origins of social inequality]. Paris: Société d'Ethnographie, Université Paris X-Nanterre, 1982.

Thomas, Rosalind. *Herodotus in Context*. New York: Cambridge University Press, 2000.

Thomson, George. *The First Philosophers: Studies in Ancient Greek Society*. London: Lawrence and Wishart, 1955.

Thucydides. *The History of the Peloponnesian War*. Translated by Richard Crawley. In *Herodotus–Thucydides*. Great Books of the Western World. Chicago: University of Chicago Press, 1952.

Weber, Max. *The Sociology of Religion*. Translated by Ephraim Fischoff. Boston: Beacon, 1964.

Xenophon. *Memorabilia*. Edited by D. C. Marchant. Medford, MA: Tufts University Perseus Digital Library. http://www.perseus.tufts.edu/hopper/text?doc=Perseus:text:1999.01.0208.

Yamakawa, Hideya. *Kodai girishia no shisô* [Ancient Greek thought]. Tokyo: Kodansha, 1993.

Index

Bergson, Henri, 1–2, 92
Bible. *See* Old Testament
biblical prophets, 1, 6
Bloch, Ernst, 60–61
bonded servitude, and Athenian
   citizenship, 41, 106
Bruno, Giordano, 61
Buddha, 1, 8, 11

cause, 39, 58–59, 90; final cause
   (*see also* Ionian philosophy: telos),
   60, 63; four forms in Aristotle,
   60, 62–64, 91; natural cause of
   afflictions, 38, 40–42
Chaos, relation to non-mythical
   thinking, 51, 58–59, 90–91
China: free thinking in, 1, 9; state
   form, 12, 13
clan societies, 1–3, 9, 12, 15, 21–24,
   35–36, 45, 49, 138–39
Cleisthenes, reforms of, 17, 21,
   103–4
city-state: European Middle Ages, 27,
   60; general form, 3, 5, 9, 13, 20, 51,
   69; struggle among, 9, 13, 20, 22,
   51, 80–81, 104–5. *See also* polis
colonies: in Americas, 28–31; in
   Iceland, 28; in Ionia, 23, 24, 27, 35,
   44, 50; relation to mobility, 68, 118
commodity exchange, 2, 12, 71,
   135–36, 148n7, 149n16. *See also*
   modes of exchange; mode C
Confucius, 1, 8–10
Cornford, F. M., 59, 75
corporeality, 126
cosmopolitanism, 37; in Diogenes, 36;
   and foreigners resident in Athens,
   101–2; in Heraclitus, 86; in Kant,
   116; in Socrates, 36, 37, 116
council form, 26, 29, 31–32, 48
covenant community: in the Ionian
   polis, 15, 22; in Judaism in age of
   Babylon, 5–7
Critias, 111
Crito, 125
Croton, 69, 71, 76, 84
Cynics: inheritance of Socrates,

36–37, 42, 79, 124; inversion of
   public and private in, 115–16

Daimon, 113, 114, 118–22, 133
Daoism, 9, 143n6
Darwin, and natural philosophy,
   64–67, 147n19
death, 52, 83, 93, 120; in Confucius,
   9; Jesus and, 152n29; in Plato,
   125–33; in Pythagoras, 69–70;
   Socrates and, 36, 86, 109–16, 124
Delian League, 17, 104, 106
demagogues, 33, 104, 110, 117, 153n40
democracy, 45; Athenian, 14, 17–21,
   26, 32, 41, 69, 75, 78, 80, 104–8;
   direct democracy of council, 31;
   modern liberal, 16, 26, 38; relation
   to taxation and redistribution,
   15–16, 72; vs. *isonomia*, 12, 14, 15
Democritus, 37, 38, 60, 64, 67, 79,
   99–102
Derrida, Jacques, 153n41
despotic state, 3, 5, 12–13, 22, 46,
   49–53, 104, 128, 129, 133, 136
dialogue, vs. monologue in Socrates,
   75, 108, 122–25
Diodorus, 64
Diogenes (the Cynic), 36–37, 115–16,
   124–25
Diogenes Laërtius, 36, 70, 89, 111, 123
Dionysius II, and Plato, 124
dual world, 72–78; in Athenian state,
   123, 131, 133; in Marx, 73; in Nietzsche, 72; in Plato, 84, 133; in Pythagoras, 72–74, 76, 78, 89, 122, 131

economic base, 1–4, 135
Egypt, 24, 42–44, 47, 69, 73; mathematics and technology in, 12, 39,
   54, 76; state form, 5, 52
Eleatics, 87, 88, 92, 93, 96–98, 108,
   122
Elenchos, 45, 93, 108
Empedocles, 64, 96–100; fables
   concerning, 100–102
empire, 1, 4, 45–47, 52, 86, 102,
   114–16, 137–39 (*see also* world

empire); Athenian, 17, 101, 103–7, 110; Lydian, 15, 80; Persian, 7, 17, 38, 80, 105; Roman, 23

Ephesus, 80–86, 89

Epicurus, 37, 67, 79, 116

equality: freedom and, 15, 16, 29, 30, 132, 139; in clan society, 18, 135; *isonomia* and, 14–15, 18, 25, 26, 35, 41; in Pythagorean Order, 71, 75; in Sparta, 16

ethnocentrism, and historiography, 43–44

European city-states, 26–28

Farrington, Benjamin, 63–65

fixed settlements, 24, 26; accumulation and, 3, 138; disparities in wealth and, 28

freedom, relation to equality, 14–16, 25, 29, 30, 32, 38, 72, 80, 130, 133

gift, and reciprocity, 2–3, 6, 22, 135

god: as idealistic agency, 59, 60, 63, 66; One God in natural philosophy, 62, 84, 85, 91, 93, 127; transcendental, 5, 7, 52, 53

gods: abandonment of, 6, 28; coercion of, 3–5, 9; of Olympus, 22, 47–50, 74, 106; rejection of in natural philosophy, 8, 28, 36, 40, 46, 56, 74, 94, 133; tribal or tutelary, 4, 5, 22, 55, 112–13

Gong Sun Longzi (Logicians), 9

Gorgias, 100, 108–9

Greek philosophy. *See* Athenian philosophy; Ionian philosophy

Han Feizi (Legalists), 9

Hecataeus, 44

Hegel, G. W. F., 100, 117; *History of Philosophy*, 31, 78, 88, 92–93; interpretation of Heraclitus, 88; Ionian philosophy and, 31; interpretation of Pythagoras, 78–79; interpretation of Parmenides, 88, 92; interpretation of Socrates, 119–20, 124; interpretation of Solon, 18–19

Hellenism, 86, 106

helots, Spartan state and, 20

Heraclitus: fire as Arche, 59, 82; Parmenides and, 87–89, 101; Pythagoras and, 83–85; relation to polis, 80–83; similarity to Socrates, 86

Herodotus, 17, 25, 30, 38, 40–47

Hesiod, 46; historical stages in, 52, 98; origins of the gods, 51; origins of human society, 51–53

Hippocrates: ethics and, 40–42; natural philosophy and, 38–40

Homer, 12; attitude to war, 48–50; Ionia and, 46, 48, 50; rejection of the gods and, 46–48, 51

hoplite, and phalanx tactics, 20, 106–7

Hundred Schools of Thought (China), 9

Icelandic Commonwealth, *isonomia* in, 26–29, 33

Icelandic sagas, comparison to Homer, 27–29

idealism, 146n5; in Plato, 79, 116; in Pythagoras, 78

indirect proof, 87, 95, 108, 123; as method of the Eleatics, 89, 91, 93–94; prior to the Eleatics, 87, 94; in Socrates, 122

inequality, and democracy, 35, 69, 133

Ionian dialect, 12, 46

Ionian philosophy, 35, 41–48, 56–67, 71–103 (*see also* natural philosophy); atomic theory and, 67; attitudes to labor in, 53, 54; cosmopolitanism and, 44, 55, 101–2; ethics and, 38, 41; evolution and, 63–65; *isonomia* and, 38, 57, 80; market economy in, 74, 76, polis form and, 37, 41, 55, 60, 68, 80–83, settlers and the colony form, 47, 55, 56, 87, 103; subjugation to Lydia and, 31, 56, 69, 80; *telos* and, 61–63; technological innovation in, 53–55, 62–63; trade and manufacturing in, 56, 74

Ionian Revolt, 81

irrigation, bureaucratic requirements for, 47, 52

Isonomia, 12–28, 36–39, 41, 45, 51, 56–57, 68, 81–83, 90, 100, 103, 118; American townships and, 28–34; Athenian democracy and, 17–19; dual world and, 74–75, 121, 131, 133; Icelandic commonwealth and, 26–28; Ionian city-states and, 12–17, 20–25

Islamic thought, 60, 147n18

Israel, captivity in Babylon, 1, 5–7, 13–14

Israel, state form, 6–10, 13

Iwasaki, Chikatsugu, 64

Jefferson, Thomas, 32

Jesus, as ethical prophet, 7

Judaism, as universal religion, 5–7, 15

Kant, Immanuel: cosmopolitanism, 55, 137; inversion of public and private, 116; phenomena vs. illusion, 94–96; relation to Parmenides, 94–96; tripartite schema, 95–96

kenon (or void), 90, 94

kinship, 12, 21–22

Kos, 39

labor, 20–21, 25–29; agricultural, 21, 29, 63, 107; division between mental and material, 73–74, 133; manual labor and trades, 21, 25, 52–54, 118; slave labor and the Athenian state, 20, 25, 26, 28, 41, 107, 118

Laozi, 1, 8–11, 143n6

Leibniz, 66

Leucippus, 98

longue durée, 43

Macedonian empire, 106

magical thinking, 2–4, 6, 9, 40, 56, 59, 61, 75–77, 82, 100, 107, 139

major Socratic lineage, 115. *See also* Aristotle; Plato

Marcus Aurelius, 102

market: in Athens, 15–16, 25, 122; in Ionia, 26; as means of regulating exchange, 12. *See also* commodity

Marx, Karl, 22, 43, 138; dissertation on Epicurus, 67; inversion of public and private in, 117; materialism and natural philosophy, 67, 73

Marxism, and modes of production, 2, 20

mathematics, 74–77, 90, 126; astronomy and, 37, 39, 77; Babylon and, 76; Egypt and, 54; money economy and, 12; music and, 75–78; Pythagoras and, 75–77, 79, 84, 88

matter, 62, 79; Arche and, 58–60, 90, 96–97; atomist view of, 99; modern view of, 67, 99; inseparability from motion, 58–61, 67, 68, 84–85, 88, 90–91, 127, 134

Mauss, Marcel, 138

Menon, 127

Mesopotamia, state form, 12, 39, 41, 47, 52, 54

Miletus, 23, 30, 37, 44, 46, 57, 81, 83, 107

military, and Greek polis, 20, 27, 104, 107, 109, 114

minor Socratic lineage, 115, 124. *See also* Cynics

modes of exchange: coexistence of, 100, 136; mode A, 4, 6–10, 26, 49, 135 (*see also* reciprocity; tribal society); mode B, 2–4, 7, 9, 26, 49, 135–36 (*see also* ruler-ruled, state); mode C, 2, 4, 7, 71, 135–36 (*see also* commodity exchange); mode D, 4, 7, 10, 26, 121, 135–40 (recuperation of A at higher level; *see also* universal religion)

modes of production, 2, 31, 43, 54, 71, 135, 139

money economy: development in Ionia, 12, 15, 20, 25–26, 76; dismantling of earlier modes of exchange, 4, 20, 25, 136, 139; penetration

to Athens, 15, 20, 25–26, 36; in
Sparta, 15, 20, 25
Mozi, 9
Mycenaean civilization, 48–50; state
form, 13

natural philosophy: critique of
religion and, 8, 28, 36, 40, 46, 51,
52, 57, 74, 91, 127; ethics and, 35,
38, 41, 80; evolution and, 63–64;
original substance and, 57, 58, 82,
85, 88–89; *physis* and, 38, 40–42,
45, 69; polis and, 37, 38, 56, 80, 83,
108; relation to breeding, 66; relation to practical arts, 53, 55, 62, 63,
74; self-movement of matter and,
58–62, 69, 88; social philosophy
and, 9, 31, 36, 55, 57, 75, 82–83;
Socrates and, 112, 121
Nietzsche, 34, 72, 134
nomadic society, 3, 5–7, 10, 24, 26,
44, 54, 138–39
nomos, 9, 40–45, 86, 109
North American colonies: *isonomia* in,
26–28; tribal societies, 23–24

Old Testament, compilation of, 5–8
oligarchy, 104, 110
Olympic games, 24, 47, 52
One, 93, 98; Heraclitus and, 85–86;
multiplicity born from, 85, 88,
96–97; Parmenides and, 89–92
Origin stories: political projection in,
7–8, 14, 28, 64, 73
original substance. *See* Arche
Orphism, 70–71

Parmenides, 87–101; indirect proof
and, 89, 91, 122; relation to Heraclitus, 87–90, 101; relation to Kant,
94–96; relation to Pythagorean
thought, 91–93, 96
patrimonial bureaucratic state, 44,
49, 51, 54
Peisistratus, 18–19, 21, 33, 69, 103
Peloponnesian War, 42, 112, 114;

aristocratic and democratic factions
in, 106, 110, 121; end of Athenian
Empire, 104, 106, 110; Thirty
Tyrants, 104
Pericles, 12, 17, 36, 105–8, 110
Persian Empire, 7, 21, 24; in the
Histories, 42–46; Ionian cities
and, 17, 30–31, 38–39; relation to
subjugated states, 17, 31, 45–46
Persian War, 42, 53, 105
Phaedo, 11, 70, 125
philosopher-king, 75, 86, 116, 127–33,
153n40; Dionysius II as, 129; and
Pythagorus, 130–31
physics: classical, 37, 62–64; modern,
66–67, quantum, 67
physis, 9, 40–48, 109, 125; as governing social behavior, 38, 40–42, 45,
48, 68; in Herodotus, 45; in Hippocrates, 40; in Homer, 48; medicine
and, 40; in Pythagoras, 68, 78
Plato, 42, 59–63, 70–77, 80–86,
112–16, 125–33; Athenian politics
and, 75, 115, 116, 127–28; attitude
to democracy, 80, 81, 125, 128, 131,
132; dialogue, 108, 124–26; dual
world and, 70, 84, 116; experience
in Syracuse, 129; idealism in, 77,
79, 116; ideas, theory of, 79, 91,
124–25, 132; inversion of Socrates
in, 42, 86, 112, 115, 116, 126–28,
131, 134; itinerant period, 75,
129–30; relation to Ionian thought,
59, 63, 65, 87, 127, 131; relation
to Pythagoras, 70, 77, 84, 86, 93,
127–30; *Seventh Letter*, 128
Plutarch, 97, 148n8
Poiesis, 63
polis (*see also* individual poleis:
Athens; Elea; Ephesus; Miletus;
Samos; Sparta), 14, 47, 49, 82, 86,
100–102, 113, 123–24; Athenian,
13, 36–38, 105–8; class antagonism within, 15, 20; comparison
to American townships, 29–31;
comparison to Icelandic common-

polis (*continued*)
    wealth, 27–29; Ionian, originality
    of, 22–23, 26, 29, 37–38, 44, 57;
    principles of, 12, 22, 27, 41, 55, 68,
    100; relation to Heraclitus, 81–82,
    86; relation to Pythagoras, 69–71;
    relation to Socrates, 86, 115–16,
    123–24; relation to Thales, 37, 69;
    social contract and, 22, 35, 55–57
Polycrates: tyranny and, 57, 69, 72,
    75, 130
Popper, Karl, 80–81, 153n40
practical arts, social status of, 41, 62,
    76, 77, 93
priesthood, 3, 7, 27, 54–55, 73–74,
    76, 140
prophet, ethical vs. exemplary, 6–10,
    11, 101
Protagoras, 108–9, 127
psychoanalysis, analogy to Socratic
    method, 124
public vs. private, in Athens, 113–24,
    128–31, 133
Pythagoras, 57, 69–78, 85–90,
    126–30; Asian thought and, 70,
    73; coinage and, 76, 148n7; Croton
    and, 69, 71–72, 76; dual world and,
    73, 74, 76, 78, 88, 122, 131; esoteric
    community and, 72; influence on
    Plato, 70, 75, 86, 93, 125, 128, 130;
    Ionia and, 57, 68, 71, 74–75, 85–87;
    itinerant period, 69, 75, 130; music
    and, 76–78; number as Arche,
    77–78, 85, 88, 97, 126; Polycrates
    and, 57, 68, 72, 130; transmigration
    and, 68–72, 76, 127
Pythagorean order, 86–89, 92, 125,
    130; city of Croton and, 70–72, 75,
    84; Plato's philosopher-king and,
    127, 129

reciprocity (*see also* modes of
    exchange; Mode A), 2–6, 21, 24,
    48–50, 135, 136, 138, 139
religion, 10, 12, 40, 51, 54, 56, 107,
    109, 130, 135, 140, 143, 146; static

and dynamic, 2–3; universal, 1,
    4–8, 136, 139, world religion, 2, 8
Republic, The, 42, 86, 127
return of the repressed, 121, 138
revolution, 1, 19, 28–33, 80, 143, 144
ruler-ruled relation (*see also* modes of
    exchange; Mode B), 2–3, 14, 26, 41,
    49, 57, 82, 135

Samos, 57, 69, 71, 72, 86, 130, 142
Schmitt, Carl, 16
Seki, Hirono, 50
servitude, Greek polis and, 15, 18, 20,
    25, 81, 106, 141
slavery, Athens and, 38, 41, 42, 44, 54,
    106, 109; Sparta and, 20, 106
society, open and closed, 1–4
Socrates, 1, 34, 86, 112–23; as a
    character in Aristophanes, 112, 119,
    as character in Platonic dialogues,
    75, 115, 125–27, 130–31; charge of
    corrupting youth, 109–10, 112–14;
    and the daimon, 113–14, 118–22,
    133; as enigma to contemporaries,
    111, 114–18; and ethical thinking,
    11, 35, 121; and immortality of
    the soul, 124, 125, inheritance
    through Plato and Aristotle (*see also*
    major Socratics), 1, 35–36, 116, 133,
    inheritance through Antisthenes,
    Diogenes and the Cynics (*see also*
    minor Socratics), 36–37, 42, 79,
    124; inversion of public and private,
    113–18, 119–23, 133, military ser-
    vice, 121; and natural philosophy,
    121, 122, 131; as pre-Socratic, 131,
    134; relation to gods of the polis,
    109, 113–18, 122; relation to the
    polis, 86, 113, 115, 124; as Sophist,
    36, 109, 112; trial and execution of,
    75, 109–14, 119, 126, 128, 131
Socratic method, 121–25
Solomon, 5–6, 13
Solon, reforms of, 18–19, 22, 25, 103,
    106, 133
Sophists, 89; position in Athens, 42,

102, 107–8, 109, 110, 113; and rule
by rhetoric, 107, 112, 113; Socrates
as, 36
soul, 38, 102, 121, 124, 125; in Plato,
70, 131; in Pythagoras, 69–72,
76, 78
Sparta, 15, 16, 22, 105–10, 111; democracy in, 20, 21; and Peloponnesian
War, 106, 110; slavery in, 20, 25,
106; relation to surrounding states,
20, 105, 106
Spinoza, 61
Statesman (Plato), 109, 131
Stoics, relation to Cynics, 102, 116
substance, original, 57–60, 64, 97,
99, 146n5. *See also* Arche; matter
superstructure, ideological, 1
Syracuse, Plato's experience in, 87,
124, 129

technology: coining, 12; in Ionia, 37,
41, 53–54, 63; lack of innovation
under Athens, 41, 53, 63; legacy
of Egypt, Mesopotamia, 12, 55, 74;
mathematics, 86
teleology: in Aristotle, 60–63, 64,
66–67; in Darwin, 66, 147n19; in
natural philosophy, 91, 98, 127; in
Plato, 123, 127
Testart, Alain, 23–24
Thales, 1, 30–31, 37–39, 53, 55–60,
64, 69, 74, 76, 81–82, 97
theology, 66–67, 73; and Plato, 60,
133–34
theoretical arts, 54, 62, 89–90
Thirty Tyrants, Athenian politics and,
104, 110–11, 128

Thomas, Rosalind, 38, 45
Thucydides, 17, 42, 43, 145n9
Timaeus, 127
tribal society, 3–7, 13, 24, 27–28, 47,
66, 73; in Athens, 21, 23, 105; nomadic confederation, 6; persistence
of tribal customs, 12, 15, 22, 55;
severing of in Ionia, 15, 18, 22–23,
55, 57, 80; tribal confederacy, 5, 12,
137–38
tribute, relation to state and, 3, 29, 53,
105, 136
tyranny, 38, 41, 109, 132–33; democracy in Athens and, 18–19, 21, 33,
103–4, 110–11, 128, 129; Pythagoras
in Samos and, 57, 69, 72–75, 86,
130; under Persian rule, 17, 39, 46,
56, 80–81; Zeno and, 89–90, 101

universal religion, 1, 4–8, 136–40

Wallerstein, Immanuel, 137
warrior-farmer, 21–24, 34, 49, 53
Weber, Max, 4, 7–8, 47, 53, 143n1
world empire, 1, 4, 47, 86, 137–38
world system, 137–38
writing systems, 37, 46; phonetic, 12,
74; priestly caste and, 7, 76

Xenophanes, 62, 87, 89, 93; critique
of anthropomorphic God, 84–85

Yamakawa, Hideya, 81, 93

Zeno, 88, 98, 116; the paradoxes,
91–93, 122; radical tendencies in,
89–90, 100–101